the KODAK Workshop Series

The Art of Seeing

the KODAK Workshop Series

The Art of Seeing

The KODAK Workshop Series

Helping to expand your understanding of photography

The Art of Seeing

Written by Derek Doeffinger

Book Design: Bill Buckett Associates, Inc.

Front Cover Design: Daniel Malczewski

Cover Photograph: Tom Beelmann

Picture Research: William S. Paris

Uncredited photographs are from the files of
Eastman Kodak Company.

Consumer/Professional & Finishing Markets
Eastman Kodak Company
Rochester, New York 14650

KODAK Publication KW-20
CAT 144 2250
Library of Congress Catalog Card Number 83-81295
ISBN 0-87985-305-0
5-84-CE New Publication
Printed in the United States of America

The Kodak materials described in this book are available from those dealers normally supplying Kodak products. Other materials may be used, but equivalent results may not be obtained.

KODAK, KODACOLOR, KODACHROME, HOBBY-PAC,
TRI-X and EKTACHROME are trademarks.

INTRODUCTION

The problem with seeing is that it is so easy and natural that we never give it a second thought. We look. We see. What could be simpler? But behind that simple act lies a profound process that affects how we act, think, learn, and how we photograph.

We learned seeing early in life. And the seeing we learned was one that would help us survive. One that would spot mother's face, charging sisters, and unlicked bowls of frosting. One that would help us avoid speeding cars and guide us down stairs. Not one that would help us photograph.

At first we paid attention to everything we saw because everything was new and interesting. Cupboard knobs, pebbles, leaves were all given their due. But eventually they became old hat and boring. So we learned to ignore. After the first few years of life, we ignored more than we saw, and our seeing became casual and uneventful. Our ways of seeing were set.

Sometime later in life we put a camera to eye and began photographing. What did we photograph? We photographed what appealed to our habits of casual seeing. We photographed things we thought were supposed to be photographed because we had seen similar photographs in magazines and books. And our results were not works of art but snapshots caught by an eye not yet trained aesthetically, an eye not yet in tune with the camera.

When dissatisfied with our results, we often sought solutions in new lenses and filters or in special techniques like panning. We avoided the real solution—ourselves. Seldom does a photograph succeed because of unusual technique or exotic equipment. It succeeds for one reason. Because the photograph was well seen.

This book will help you see to photograph. It will put you in harmony with your camera. You and the camera will function as one.

It will help you overcome habits of ordinary seeing. It will help you understand the ways of your seeing and how those ways can be altered. It will rekindle your awareness of the many things to be photographed. It will show you the visual aspects to look for in a scene and how light arbitrates appearance. It will make you reexamine preconceptions and prejudices about what and how to photograph.

But most of all it will help you see the things only you can see.

Robert W. Carder

Contents

Preconceptions

Admit it or not, you have preconceptions. We all have them. They are unavoidable. In the depths of the mind they glide, unseen in the darkness, unheard in the silence, waiting. At the sight of a flower, a face, or any other photographic bait, preconceptions wheel in unison like a school of mackerel and carry you along unawares. Elusive and intangible, preconceptions always agree, always flatter, never complain, never criticize. They make photography a breeze. They free you from the sweat of thought, liberate you from the mental calisthenics that leave the brain weary, the mind sore, the imagination puffing. Buoyed by preconceptions, you have only to pose the subject ("Smile"), snap the shutter ("Hold still"), and pat yourself on the back ("Way to go, fella"). Why evict such agreeable creatures? Because they inhibit your photography.

We expect photographs to look a certain way and to contain certain subjects. When they don't, our first reaction is rejection. But an important part of seeing is the suspension of knee jerk reactions and a reexamination of what a photograph is, what it can be.

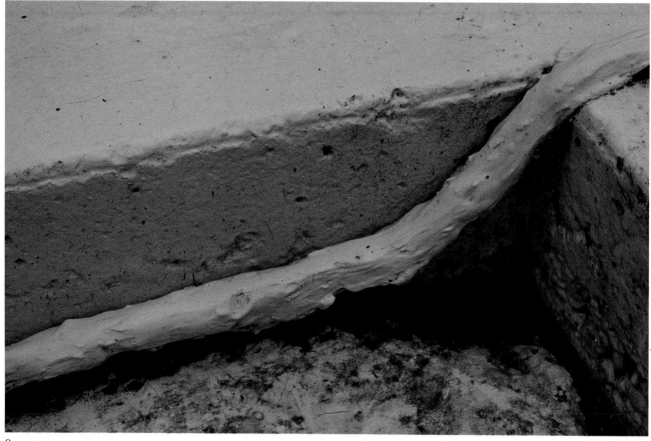

Sprinklers are one of those things not often photographed. But this sprinkler, photographed with the backlight of an evening summer sun, seems to symbolize the quiet business of suburbia. The rich hues of KODACHROME 64 Film add to the mood.

PHOTOGRAPHIC PRECONCEPTIONS

A photographic preconception is a preformed opinion you have about photography. You may be aware of the preconception; more often you are not.

Preconceptions take many forms. You might have preconceptions about where to photograph. Have you ever taken a picture in your bathroom? At the supermarket? At work?

You might have preconceptions about when to photograph. Have you ever photographed at night? In the rain? At twilight?

You might have preconceptions about what and how to photograph. Have you ever photographed a shoe? A beer bottle? The stem of a flower but not the flower? Do you photograph only pretty things like flowers and waterfalls?

Coming to grips with your preconceptions is the first step towards better seeing. In *Looking at Photographs,* John Szarkowski writes:

Photography, if practiced with high seriousness, is a contest between a photographer and the presumptions of approximate and habitual seeing. The contest can be held anywhere—on a city sidewalk, or in a scientific laboratory, or among the markers of ancient dead gods.

FORMATION OF PRECONCEPTIONS

Before grappling with preconceptions, you should know more about them. How do they form? Why do they form?

Photographic preconceptions start forming early in life. In the first hour after my daughter's birth, I thrust before her unfocusing eyes a picture of herself in her mother's arms.

Within a week, I would show her a storybook full of pictures. Within a month, wheeled through the supermarket, she would glimpse 30,000 products, many with pictures on the labels. Within a year, she would chortle at the boy on the cereal box and wave at the baby on the diaper box. And in the years ahead she would leaf through magazines and see ads showing toilet cleaners, deodorants, and cars sparkling and appealing.

With each passing image registering on her eyes, neural pathways became established, automatically sorting and shuttling faces on this route, flowers on that, and before she would ever take a picture, thousands, even millions of images would further wear the visual pathways.

And she saw the things pointed out by her parents. One parent might show her the breezy dance of tulips, the other a carburetor. Her future ways of seeing would, in part, depend on what she was taught to appreciate.

And, in part, her ways of seeing would depend on the culture, the society in which she grew. A Chinese child would see a different world and be taught to see differently within that world than would an American child. Differences would exist within the same culture. A child growing up beneath crowded skyscrapers and within the blare of horns and stench of exhaust fumes would see differently than one growing up isolated on a plain where the eye is unbounded and the sounds are of silence and the smells of earth.

So has your seeing been shaped by parents and culture. When you took your first picture, the photographic knowledge buried in your mind seeped to the surface and guided your seeing. Now you are consciously seeking knowledge of photography by reading a book. And it is loaded with the preconceptions of the people who put it together. Only now you are forewarned.

What did you learn from other photography books? Enough to know how to compose a picture? Enough to know the pitfalls of a slow shutter speed? Enough to be channeled into procedures and beliefs that may inhibit your photography?

Until now you have learned from others. Now you must learn from yourself and see for yourself.

Robert Stahl

WHAT IS A SUBJECT?

Most simply put, a subject is what you photograph. In other words, a subject can be anything and anything can be a subject. But few photographers believe that. They impose restrictions as to subjects proper for photography. From photographs they have seen in books and magazines, they form definite notions as to what sort of things are proper subjects for photographs (curiously, the books or magazines seldom suggest only certain subjects are proper).

Why impose restrictions where there are none? Instead of photographing things you think you're sup-

posed to photograph, photograph what interests you. You are your most powerful resource; so don't waste time photographing what interests others unless it also interests you. Your way of life, your opinions, your surroundings belong only to you. Trash cans upended in an alley, your spouse sprinkling the lawn, suds settling in the sink, a grocery cart dripping with rain—what you choose to photograph reveals your psyche, your outlook, a unique way of seeing—your way. Photographer Bob Llewellyn puts it best, "Every photograph you make is a self-portrait."

D. H. Lawrence wrote, ". . . So

much depends on one's attitude. One can shut many, many doors of receptivity in oneself; or one can open many doors that are shut."

Have you been receptive to the world around you? Review your photography to see what you consider to be subjects. Are you unnecessarily limiting yourself? Do you photograph only conventional subjects like sailboats, flowers, and people? Have you ever photographed a washcloth, a tub, a tree root, an abstract of leaves? Why not? Edward Weston found "beauty" in a bedpan. Irving Penn found it in cigarette butts. Pete Turner found it in a trash can.

10

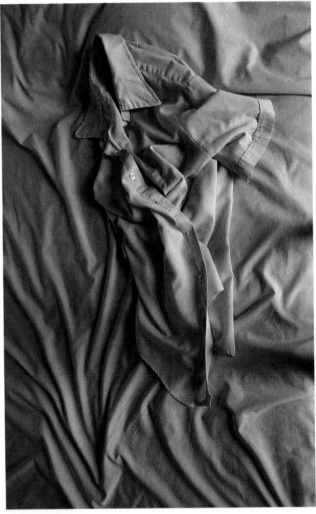

HOW SHOULD A SUBJECT APPEAR IN A PHOTOGRAPH?

From the photographs we have seen and taken, we evolve definite ideas of how a subject should appear in a photograph. In focus, unobscured, properly exposed, easily identifiable, idealized (flower at its peak as opposed to wilted): these are some of the qualities we expect to see.

But these qualities can be preconceptions. Why unvaryingly heed such edicts? Although most photographs should be in focus and correctly exposed, all need not be if you can create an interesting unfocused or overexposed image.

Nor need you always clearly show the subject or show it so it is easily identifiable. The photographs on this spread show the benefits of overcoming preconceptions about the appearance of a subject in a photograph.

To preserve the sparkling brightness of a milkweed seed in a dewy meadow, the photographer overexposed slide film by one stop. The out-of-focus sun was made large by using a large f/stop, f/3.5.

Jim Brandenberg

By panning at the slow shutter speed of 1/2 second, the photographer made a ghostly and delicate image of a swan. To obtain slow shutter speeds, shoot under dim light, use a slow-speed film such as KODACHROME 25 Film, or reduce light reaching the film with a polarizing or neutral density filter.

Robert Llewellyn

Most photographers show subjects clearly. But Llewellyn purposely chose a viewpoint placing a tangle of branches in front of the Capitol building—perhaps to suggest the tangle of politics.

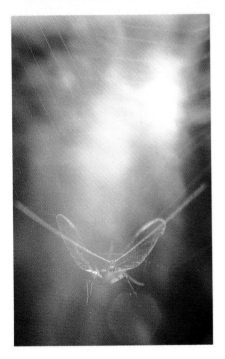 

In these two pictures flare was used creatively. For the web-trapped bug, flare acts as a powerful source of energy. In the other picture, it simply forms a pattern of hexagons caused by the diaphragm in the lens.

SHOULD A SUBJECT BE THE SUBJECT?

To a degree hard to measure and hard to understand, language influences how we reason and, therefore, how we photograph. For instance, in photography we repeatedly come across the term subject. In the English language and the language of photography, we usually think of a subject as some object, some thing—a barn, a boat, a person.

The focus on things is reinforced by our culture. We are surrounded by things. Calculators, woks, roller skates, stereos, flea collars, and thousands of other things abound. So given the tilt by language and society, it may be excusable to subconsciously think of photographic subjects as things.

But photographs need not be of distinct things. They can be of washes of color, sprays of light, arrangements of shapes, progressions of tones. They can even be of conglomerations of things without making one thing central, without placing one particular subject so it is identified as the thing photographed. Instead, the picture can draw power from all rather than one, as in the street scene by Lee Friedlander.

Making "subjectless" pictures can be hard. Viewers used to having the subject waved under their noses may balk when no single subject greets them. Should the viewer indulge you, then you must come through and find a scene in which disparate elements unite to say one thing.

Although most of us photograph scenes we find, some photographers must fabricate. They must invent their own realities. They do so by making collages of drawings and blueprints and hairbrushes, or by building exotic papier maché figures and then photographing them. They construct whatever suits their purposes, and then photograph their constructions.

These photographers are expressing ideas and concepts not easily stated by photographing found things. Their photographs may seem unconventional, especially when first seen. They may even seem absurd to those accustomed to seeing pictures of the world around them. But many of their pictures are interesting, because like a riddle or a crossword puzzle, they challenge the viewer to solve the logic behind them. Others are simply visually entertaining, and some simply don't work.

But all show that photography need not be limited by traditions and preconceptions as to what is a subject.

Pete Turner/The Image Bank

By overcoming the
inclination to think of
photographs as
pictures of individual
things, these three
photographers were
able to see differently.
Opposite page, Pete
Turner found an
abstract design in a
boat wake. Lee
Friedlander, **right,**
found an entertaining
intersection. Bill
Paris, **below,** who
doesn't trust the found
to express his feelings,
built this contraption
and photographed it
(the zigzag of light is
from a swinging
flashlight).

Lee Friedlander

Bill Paris

15

HOW THINGS LOOK

We know how things look. Or think we do. Imagine a tree, a flower, a car. The mental images we conjure are probaly quite similar, harking back to early childhood when mother held us in her lap and pointed to the page and said, "That's a tree," and traced her finger from trunk to branches.

From the very beginning the mind, faced with a welter of shapes, forms and colors, sought to simplify. It did so by classifying differences and similarities. For each of the hundreds of common objects, it sketched the difference or similarities into a few mental images that stood for tree, flower, car, house, chair. By being reductive, by making one stand for many, the mind found it easier to remember and comprehend.

The danger is that we may photograph according to those stereotypes. A tree, a flower, a car—don't simply see the images trapped by the mind. See things not how they have looked but how they might look. Envision possibilities. Imagine. Work at imagining.

A tree, a flower, a car, a lighthouse, a person, a horse—we know how these things are supposed to look but here they break the stereotypes.

17

OVERCOMING PRECONCEPTIONS

Facing preconceptions can be painful. Why? Because you are questioning your values, your logic—no easy thing—but you must do it.

Review your photographs, looking for patterns of subjects, viewpoints, camera technique. What is good about your photography? What needs work? If you have trouble being objective about your work (and most of us do), ask a friend (even if your friend knows little about photography) to look at and talk about your photographs. A friend won't have your prejudices and may enlighten you. Be a stern self-critic and do as Ralph Hattersley suggests: "Photographers [should] observe themselves as observers and in that way come to understand why they see the way they do."

Practice seeing subjects in new ways. Instead of seeing the horseness of a horse, you might see it as a landscape—the prairie of its back rising into a mountainous neck. Or you might see it as a temple supported with four slender columns. Instead of seeing the flowerness of a flower, you might see it as a dancer and wait for the breeze to create a whir of color, or you might see it as a wine glass and show the stem joining the cup.

Free your imagination. Photograph one subject in as many ways as possible. At dawn, at midday, from above, from below, blurred, sharp, from close up, from far away, in focus, out of focus, correctly exposed, overexposed, with camera steady, with camera jiggled, in the summer, in the winter, centered, uncentered, and on and on.

RULES

Some preconceptions result because we automatically follow rules. From the delivery room to the burial plot we have been indoctrinated to observe rules and regulations—written and unwritten. Pay at the checkout counter. Drive on the right side of the road. Don't stare at people.

Photography is no exception to the rule: Hold the camera steady; expose properly; frame vertically for tall subjects, horizontally for wide subjects; focus accurately.

Following rules has its benefits in that you can predict the results and avoid unpleasant surprises like car crashes and food poisoning. But in photography if you slavishly follow rules, you often miss out on the pleasant surprises that come from breaking them.

What happens if you leap into the air while photographing an ocean wave or greatly overexpose a backlighted grove of trees? The results may be as revealing as they are unpredictable.

Rules are guidelines. Don't become a slave to them. Experiment and break every rule you can think of, even if you must do it in the most outrageous manner possible. Try to predict the results and view the results with an open mind, accepting what pleases you and rejecting what displeases you.

Karin Rosenthal

In the vision of the photographer, human forms and earth forms are one.

RESISTANCE AND FAILURE

We all resist change. That is natural. Our resistance is a way of affirming our beliefs, whereas accepting change suggests our beliefs were wrong. None of us wants to think we were wrong.

Resistance also lets us proceed along familiar paths, and familiarity is comfortable. Uncertainty upsets. To accept change means to meet with uncertainty, but it also means to learn. So reduce your resistance. In primitive countries, farmers fertilize fields by burning them. Burn your resistance and watch the lush fields grow.

We may not realize it, but the urge to conform and fear of failure may also guide our seeing. Thus, we see and photograph things already approved as photogenic, already accepted as "good" photographic subjects.

We photograph the daffodils, not the garbage bag; the leaf, not the sidewalk. And rather than photograph them in a difficult manner, we opt for the easy way that will produce results and be acceptable to others.

Our society frowns upon failure. As part of that society we don't want to be frowned upon—even though a failure in photography may be as innocuous as a blurred, rather silly-looking picture. Does fear of failure ever enter into your photography? If not, you are one of the lucky ones. If so, overcome it. Don't be afraid to fail. Embrace it. Failure means you are growing, striving, learning, that you are trying to shatter your assumptions.

A tree filled with lovers' carvings embraced by another tree inspired the photographer with thoughts of arboreal sympathy for human love. It doesn't work. What did the photographer suffer? The loss of a frame of film.

Few photographers would dare be so simple as to show but a field of snow and a distant row of trees. But Shinzo Maeda's simple vision produces a stunning photograph.

Shinzo Maeda/The Image Bank

Awareness

Twenty thousand feet in the air. Returning from New York City. He watched as stewardesses and stewards squeezed through the aisle with a cart of snacks, listened as cellophane and snap tops burst into a staccato of small explosions. Watched as passengers unfolded trays, listened as plastic cups clicked. Watched as passengers pressed back and stewardesses reached across.

Ginger ale, no ice. The plane, headed west by northwest, banked and dipped. The sun streamed into the window. The photographer noticed, reached under his seat and extracted his camera. He framed. He focused. He shot, and shot again. The bzzt of the power winder filled the air. Heads turned. What was he doing? The observer was now the observed. He slumped into his seat for a better angle, held firm as the plane bounced in an air pocket, held firm as a steward brushed by, held firm, then released the shutter to capture the flare of a rainbow from sunlight stabbing his soft drink. Awareness.

The photographer used a large aperture, f/4, to achieve selective focus. Slow- and medium-speed films, such as KODACHROME 64 Film or KODACOLOR VR 100 Film, are good choices when using selective focus in bright light.

Brian A. Vikander

Jean Anderson

*Snow accenting the arch of a doorway,
light transforming river scum into a
galaxy. Although neither event
is uncommon, the photographers'
alertness was.*

Because simple awareness gets in the way of doing things, we screen out more than we see. But in photography, the more you see the more you can photograph. So your first goal is to become more aware of your surroundings. Look at things, even minor things—especially minor things—and you will see more.

Practice increasing your simple awareness. At work set aside a few minutes to study your desk. See the shapes, lines, forms, colors, and arrangements of stapler, pencils, calculator, telephone. In the hallways, observe light streaming through the window. At home, look at your kitchen. See the dirty dishes in the sink, the carrot peels curling up from the stainless steel, the table legs against the linoleum. Study their visual attributes. Envision them within the borders of a photograph. Practice awareness until it becomes second nature.

THE FAMILIAR

Edward Weston said, "Anything that excites me for any reason, I will photograph: not searching for unusual subject matter, but making the commonplace unusual."

Each day you do and see many things almost subconsciously. The actions are routine, the objects involved familiar.

Each day you throw back the covers on your bed creating a series of mountain ranges and plains. The ranges of the blanket are high and steep, those of the sheet small and gentle.

Each day you glance at the bar of soap melting in the shower, the wheelbarrow filling with rain in the backyard, the cars parked along the street, the gas pumps at the service station.

Each day you pass by hundreds of scenes so familiar that you never give them a second look.

In your life the ordinary and familiar things seldom even get a first look. Thus their very power resides in their ordinariness, their familiarity. Nobody expects much if anything of them and when you are able to photograph them in a way that arouses feelings, viewers are doubly moved because these things are so commonplace. They're like the quiet kid down the street who disappears into the woodwork until one day you walk past the kid's house and hear a Bach concerto spilling forth. Who would've thought it of that kid?

Good photographs of familiar things revise thinking. They make you reconsider your surroundings.

They revive a world previously dead to your senses. Who would've thought that the frosted folds of a garbage bag would make a good photograph? Who would've thought that a clothespin on a clothesline would make a good photograph?

Who would have thought that the clothes basket in the bedroom would glow in the morning light? In photographing the familiar you may find that a razor can be as evocative as a sunset, maybe more so because it's personal and common, an emblem of your daily life.

Although belief in the power of the familiar can rejuvenate your photography, you might, at first, have trouble finding things to photograph. Everything still looks—well ordinary. The popsicle stick belongs in the

trash. The snow on the fender needs swept away. You want to photograph, but why bother if you see things as trivial. You become frustrated.

Frustration thwarts many new skills. What can you do to overcome it? Remember, you cause your own frustration. Relax. Loosen up. Don't rush things. Don't expect too much too soon. Because it's a difficult skill, developing new awareness takes time.

Start by starting. Even if something seems trivial and indeed may be trivial, photograph it anyhow. Wait until you're alone in the house; then wander through the rooms photographing. Use a tripod or high-speed film. With KODACOLOR VR 400 and 1000 Films, you can often handhold the camera when taking existing-light pictures indoors. And they are specially sensitized to give better colors (without filtration) than normal daylight films shot under tungsten and fluorescent lighting. You may not take a single good picture the first few times but you will have achieved a great accomplishment—belief that you can see differently. Believing is seeing. Once you believe you can see differently, you will.

Utensils in a sink, **left,** *a laundry basket, feet in a tub, a frosted garbage bag and many other worthy scenes are viewed each day and ignored.*

OBSERVATION

Observation lets you become familiar with your quarry. You can observe from a distance or from nearby; you can observe at night or midday. You can observe how a subject relates to the surroundings, how the surroundings relate to it, how it relates to you. You can watch light skip over it and hide it in shadows, or flare upon it with brilliance.

The careful observer learns many things before releasing the shutter. The careless observer learns only (if then) after releasing the shutter. Although both learn, the careful observer learns faster and suffers fewer disappointments. Yet even the careful observer can't always be sure of the outcome. Will what you see show in the photograph? There's only one way to find out for sure. Photograph it. Only through much experience will your observations become reliable and insightful.

Observation deals in the here and now, not the future. You see what is before you. But before you is a figment of time and coincidence, and may not—indeed will not—look the same five hours, five weeks, five months later. The moral? Don't overlook potential.

Like a football scout, an enlightened observer should be on the lookout for potential, that raw stumbling lad who with a little work can become a star. Think of that noon drive on a road curving through a wheat field. How would that scene look at sunset, early in the morning? Think of that lone oak. How would it look with a full moon hanging over it? A crescent moon? In the blue of twilight? In the snow?

Always keep potential in mind. Always keep in mind that things can and will look different. Do you know the date of the full moon? The time the sun rises and sets? Outdoor photographers benefit by carrying a compass and noting the directions different subjects face, and imagining subjects under different lighting and weather. All photographers should temper their observations with potential. See what is as what could be.

Don't hesitate to keep notes: creative ideas, techniques, potential subjects under certain conditions. Write down anything that comes to mind. If you try keeping it all in your head, you'll forget, and if you forget, you won't get the picture. Some photographers may believe notekeeping foolish—anticreative. "Artists see and react, man." But they'll really react if they missed a picture because they forgot something. Even when without a camera, I carry a pocket notebook and jot down any stray thoughts about photography. "Orange light of setting sun on Webster water tower. Estimate sun will set on railroad tracks April 25. Dog sleeping on bed lit by windowlight." Those notes were written while grocery shopping.

Let's say it once again. Photograph, photograph, photograph, and if you don't have a camera, look, see, imagine. That's the best way to expand your awareness, to sharpen your seeing, to dilute preconceptions. Photograph things you don't usually photograph and in ways you never imagined. Force yourself to photograph differently for the sake of photographing differently. If you're a people photographer, photograph flowers or rocks. Then photograph people as you might photograph flowers or rocks. Photograph them from the rear or include just certain parts of their body. Photograph them in the least expected ways you can imagine.

Gain as many and varied experiences as you can, because your photography rises from your experiences. Those experiences should include reading a variety of photography books—fine art ones as well as how-to.

Series: Charles Brethauer

What is also can be. **Above,** *a city skyline appears dull at midday, dull at sunset, but springs to life at sunrise,* **opposite,** *when the tracks glow and the buildings are silhouetted. A tobacco-colored graduated filter was used in the large picture to darken the sky and add color.*

The glory of light and shadow

Teaser of texture, molder of form, bearer of color, instigator of sight, light makes photography. Embrace light. Admire it. Love it. But above all, study it. Glory in the fists of light exploding from a cloud covering the sun. Swing through the amber light of morning. Glide through the blue strata of twilight. Soar through the crystalline sky after a thunderstorm. See how one moment's light chisels lines clean and purges colors pure and the next moment's light buries detail in shadow. Know light. Know it for all you are worth, and you will know the key to photography.

MORE THAN ILLUMINATION

What do we see? Do we see cars and chairs, telephones and desks, buildings and roads? Or do we simply detect disturbances in the light, ripples and eddies in the flow of electromagnetic radiation, disruptions that we identify as things causing the ripples and eddies?

A paradox. Perhaps nonsensical because there's no doubt we see things. Perhaps sensible because there's no doubt we see light. Only light—not things—strikes the retina.

Physiologically, we see light—the retina measures intensities, contrasts, wavelengths, and the patterns they form. Psychologically, we see things—the brain constructs the intensities, wavelengths, and patterns into a model of reality.

In *Eye, Film, and Camera*, Ralph Evans asserts, "Perhaps the most important fact to understand about vision is the extent to which we have trained ourselves from birth to see objects rather than light."

As Evans suggests, we tend to accept light as a mere illuminator, an invisible intermediate that reveals the world of things. While we may normally see things to photograph, it is often more important to see the light, and in photography, it is of prime importance to understand that light affects appearance.

When we see a bus or a sleeping cat, we see only the light reflected from the surface of the bus or from the surface of the cat—a coincidence of light and surface. With each shift in angle of light and surface, and with each dimming of light, bus and cat appear differently. Their features remain constant. Their appearances do not. Light transforms. How would a bus look in the dark, in bright sunlight? How would a cat look on an overcast day, in twilight, against a sunset? Different each time, only because the light was different each time.

Light has several qualities that affect appearances of buses, cats, dogs, and other things. Light can raise or squelch texture, reveal or hide form, enhance or extinguish color.

In the "Light Primer" at the end of this section, we'll give you a refresher course on the qualities of light that affect appearances.

Rows of ceiling lights reflected in the floor form a corridor of light in which the people seem suspended. Shot on KODAK EKTACHROME 400 Film.

The different appearances of the scene at right result from changes in lighting.

Robert Brink

Diane Woodrum Hensley

Lighting can be an active or a passive part of a picture. Strong directional lighting is active, calls attention to itself with dark shadows and bright highlights. It alters the mood of a subject. Diffuse lighting does little more than illuminate a scene. It lets the subject stand by itself. In the picture above, harsh sidelighting energizes the angles of the building and the stride of the woman. The lighting makes the picture dynamic. In the picture at right, diffuse light reinforces the tranquility of reflections in a still stream. Strong directional light would have lessened the pervading calm.

Ernest Braun/The Image Bank

LOOKING FOR LIGHT

Many photographs are taken because the photographer liked the lighting. If the lighting isn't right, you can wait for it to change or you can look for better light. Since waiting isn't always possible, it's often wiser to look for better light.

Look for light. Look for that shaft of light slipping through branches and spotlighting the pot of geraniums on the tree stump. Look for sunlight following the storm that contrasts the farmhouse against fleeting thunderheads.

Look from the other side of those frontlighted horses to see how the backlighting riffles their manes and feathers their fetlocks.

Look for light. Walk through the city and peer into an alley and see how one building bleaches in midday sun while the building opposite inks out in shadow. Observe the interplay of light and shadow created by the fire escape. Walk into that country church and see light polish pews into a succession of curves.

Look for light. An hour before sunset, climb into your car and drive away from the setting sun. See how the glass skyscrapers shimmer and glimmer with the gold of the falling sun. At twilight, when the grain elevators and water towers darken, see how the railroad tracks glow from light in the overhead sky.

*The rain of fire, **above**, resulted from the photographer standing behind a waterfall and photographing it against the setting sun.*

SHADOW

Behind every light is shadow. The biggest shadow is night, one side of the earth shaded by the other. In photography we deal with small shadows—a cloud shadowing an orchard, an apple shadowing part of a table, a nose shadowing a cheek.

Shadows do many things—some beneficial, some not. On the good side, shadows hide, brighten, create mood. They can even be subjects. On the bad side, they confuse, obscure, distract.

Let's look at the bright side of shadows. Shadows are shapes. As shapes, they can form subjects, and if repeated they can form patterns, which also can be subjects.

Shadows also hide. Hiding can be as important as revealing. Within a given scene should you reveal more or less? Too much revelation in a photograph dilutes and distracts, bounces the eye around like a pinball. Too little revelation bores, gives nothing to entertain the eye. You can hide unwanted details in shadows—the shadow of your hand, of your body, of a cardboard, or a new shadow created by a different viewpoint.

Often shrouding, but not hiding, a face, a stairway, or other detail in a veil of shadow intrigues the eye, creates mystery, atmosphere. Try fully and partially disclosing the same shadowy scene. Which lighting fits that scene?

Light brightens. Shadow brightens. Light brightens with illumination. Shadow brightens with contrast. When seen next to a shadow, a light area seems even lighter, and the shadow seems darker. Proximity reinforces differences. To make a brilliant scene appear more brilliant, a bold color appear bolder, add some rich, deep shadows; to make a shadowy scene seem more shadowy, add a bright area.

Shadow also means to stalk stealthily, and in photography shadows stalk the photographer. Though they do so in daylight and are there for the seeing, shadows often are not noticed until seen in the photograph. In the photograph, shadows cry out when mistreated. They say look at the details you've hidden in my murkiness, look at how our patterns distract from the subject.

Overlooking shadows is natural because the irises in your eyes automatically open to let in more detail when faced with a shadow. All this happens quickly as the eye scans the scene, opening for shadows, closing for highlights, and sending signals of details in color that the brain combines into an image. In effect, you see through the shadows to pick up details the film may miss, and you miss shadows the film catches.

Just as shadows trigger your irises to open, so should they trigger your mind to open and analyze what their effects will be in a photograph. Shadow analysis is necessary because unlike the eye's ability to combine several exposures of a contrasty scene into a less contrasty mental image, the camera makes but one exposure to produce an image on film. Clearly the camera and film see contrasty scenes differently from your vision which can easily see detail throughout light ranges over 1000:1. Color prints and slides can handle a range of brightness less than 100:1. Something's got to give. Usually it's the shadows.

You can lighten shadows with a reflector, fill-in flash, or an increase in exposure. You can sometimes darken highlights by using a graduated neutral density filter over them, such as in a picture with sky. One half of this filter has clear glass. The other half has an increasingly darker tint of gray that reduces incoming light without changing the color balance. If you want both highlight and shadow detail, you must reduce the brightness range (contrast) so that the film can capture that detail. With black-and-white negative film, you can over-expose and underdevelop according to a zone system. You may also want to balance exposure between highlight and shadow detail, or lean toward the end with important detail.

Robert W. Foedisch

An inky shadow spilling across the picture plays against the well-defined shape of the porpoise and its shadow.

© Mary Laurence

Dr. Roland Maurice

Above, because the woman is seemingly bending under the weight of the light, the light seems to have a physical presence. Keeping the women in the shadow and resisting the traditional tendency to move people into bright light before photographing them required insight by the photographer.

Sometimes a shadow can form the subject of a picture. By photographing the shadow instead of the person, the photographer made a more subtle, mysterious picture.

Buck Campbell

*Bright light gives an airy, romantic feeling, **top,** and dim light **bottom,** gives a sad feeling. The blue light of skylight, **right,** increases the pensiveness of this photograph.*

MOOD

More than composition, more than form and shape, sometimes more than the subject itself, light sets the mood. And why not? Light is what registers on the film.

Foreboding, tense, gloomy, gay, sad, the moods of light tumble across the scene. Mood begins simply with quantity and then gets more complex. Lots of light cheers. Little light saddens. Warm light, the gold of a sunset, gladdens. Cold light, the blue of a rainy day, depresses. But between lots and little and warm and cold, burgeon combinations of factors like direction, harshness, contrast, and subject that can shade mood in many directions.

From a given photograph, we may be able to dissect each rib and artery of light and may even be able to show how they quicken a photograph. Yet the varieties of light are so many that we can't possibly anticipate the many moods created.

We can accept that light does help create mood and that unless we carefully observe light, we will catch only the obvious moods—the cascades of sunbeams spraying from a thunderhead or the backlighting stoking a model's mane.

But mood does not equate with drama alone. Mood can be subtle. It can be a quilt of light and shadow filtered onto a bedroom wall. It can be the highlights glimmering in the drops on the shower tiles or the yellow light of evening on a fence.

Light Primer

Since light makes subjects visible, you should know three important characteristics of light that influence your perceptions of subjects. These characteristics are direction, quality, and color.

DIRECTION

Light can come from virtually any direction, and each direction affects the appearance of a scene's three-dimensionality. The most common directions are frontlighting, sidelighting, and backlighting.

Frontlighting

Frontlighting is when the light source is behind the photographer. Direct frontlighting makes scenes look flat but readily shows shape. Cast behind subjects, shadows disappear reducing the three-dimensionality of a scene. Frontlighting excels in revealing detail.

Sidelighting

Sidelighting is when the light source is at the photographer's side. With sidelighting, shadows become apparent, raising texture and rounding out form. Sidelighting excels in revealing three-dimensionality. With harsh sidelighting, shadows may intrude. An exposure increase of 1 to 1 1/2 stops may be required to show shadow detail.

Backlighting

Backlighting is when the light source shines in the photographer's face. Backlighting can indicate distance and raise texture. With large scenes having a foreground and background, shadows cast toward the camera indicate distance. With small scenes, the shadows primarily reveal texture and secondarily distance.

QUALITY

Quality refers to harshness or softness of the lighting. Point sources, such as the sun and electronic flash, give harsh light (sharp shadows). Diffuse sources, such as an overcast sky, shade lighting, or bounce flash, give soft light (unsharp shadows).

Harsh light

The strong, directional light from the sun bleaches subtle colors and burnishes brilliant colors. It often gives hard and heavy shadows that contrast with highlights. It works well with simple and bold subjects but can overwhelm more delicate ones.

Soft light

Soft light revives subtle hues and quiets bold colors. Often directionless, it seems to come from all over. Soft shadows and dull highlights give a low contrast that works well for showing detail in busy or delicate subjects. Soft light is favored for portraits.

COLOR

Color originates from light. Midday sunlight appears colorless because it carries a nearly even mixture of all wavelengths. But the color of daylight can vary with time of day, with the weather, seasons, and latitude. Sunset is orangish. Overcast days, shade, and twilight are bluish. If a color isn't what you want, you can change it with a filter. Although tungsten lights contain a full range of wavelengths, they usually are abundant in yellow and red wavelengths. Fluorescent lights lack some wavelengths, typically red, resulting in pictures from daylight film being tinged greenish.

The eye tends to see constant color. That is, it sees white paper as white in sunlight or tungsten light, a face as face colored under a variety of light sources, even though paper and faces reflect the different colors of the light sources. As R. L. Gregory states in *Eye and Brain,* "The eye tends to accept as white not a particular mixture of colours, but rather the general illumination whatever this may be."

But film readily picks up color differences from different light sources, thus for proper coloration, film must be filtered or matched to the light source. Daylight film for daylight, tungsten film for tungsten light. Alternatively, incoming light can be filtered to provide correct colors in pictures.

Midday

Sunset

The color of daylight changes with time of day and atmospheric conditions. As these two pictures show, color of light alters the feel of a scene.

VISION AND LIGHT

By definition light is electromagnetic radiation which the eye can detect. But, electromagnetic radiation includes more than light. It includes x-rays, microwaves and radio waves, and ranges in wavelengths from a fraction of a billionth of an inch (gamma rays) to miles long (long radio waves). Light waves are about 1/50,000 of an inch long.

Nearly every form of life reacts to light. In function, the human eye reacts to light through two systems: one system for nighttime seeing, the other for daytime seeing. Rod cells lining the retina function in dim light, cone cells, the other receptors, in bright light. So sensitive is the nighttime vision that the smallest quantity of light, one quantum, causes a chemical change in a rod cell of the retina. However, it takes 5 to 10 quanta at the retina to make a chemical change large enough to create an electrical impulse that is sent to the brain resulting in the sensation of light. In perfect conditions, 5 to 10 quanta reach the retina from a candle 17 miles away.

Similarly, one quantum of light can be detected by a sensitive film, but four or more quanta are required to produce a latent image that can be developed.

Elements of the scene

Before you can find something, you have to know what you're looking for. To diagnose, a doctor looks for specific symptoms: a discoloration of fingernails, a rash on the inside of the elbow. To instruct, a golf teacher looks at the pupil's form: a stiff left arm, the shifting of weight, the track of the swing, the follow-through. What should a photographer look for? Line, shape, form, texture, color, dimension, and the subject itself—these are among the critical visual elements.

Line, shape, texture, form, and color are the parts of speech in visual language, photography in our case, that the eye and mind seek to identify the world. Common to most subjects, these traits are not always given equal importance by the mind, which tends to distill, especially when just one characteristic identifies. The key to sky may be color, to an egg, shape, and to sand, texture.

To become fluent in communicating through photography, you must become competent in linking the parts of speech—texture to form, shape to color—to make a clear, concise statement. You get but one chance. If you have to point to things in your photograph and mutter, "Look right there, see the way the tree trunk intersects the road, that's what makes it work," then the photograph doesn't work.

Like parts of speech, line, shape, color, form, and texture can be combined to say many things. You can praise, carp, clarify, or obscure. Within a photograph, you can make a potato nearly as apparent and tangible as if it were sitting atop the photograph, or you can make it as invisible and intangible as though it were underground.

HAPPENINGS

Line, shape, texture, and the rest make up what we consider aesthetic elements—if arranged pleasingly they also make up a good photograph. Sometimes, however, a subject lacks well-tuned aesthetics, yet still makes a good photograph. Why? Because it's a happening, an occurrence, an unusual event. Unusual events show things not often seen. They provide new or uncommon information and arouse the viewer's curiosity and stimulate intellect.

Shifting from the sublime to the absurd can be difficult yet should be practiced so you don't miss opportunities like these clowning brothers.

Few would argue that an authentic photograph of the Loch Ness monster or of aliens disembarking from a UFO would have great appeal, even if not aesthetically top-notch. An unusual event, however, need not be quite that unusual. It might be a dog-sled race, a hawk clutching a writhing snake, a girl performing acrobatics on her skateboard, or a spider wrapping

a grasshopper in a shroud of silk. Magazines like *Geo* and *National Geographic* enthrall readers with their events, their presentations of "eccentric" rituals and life styles in far-flung countries.

Whenever you find something qualifying as an unusual event, do your best to also exploit its aesthetic qualities.

Stephen B. Phillips

LINE

Lines can be thick or thin, long or short, straight or curved, explicit or implicit, horizontal, vertical or oblique. Lines lead, separate, connect, stabilize, and destabilize. They take many forms, as anyone knows who has ever stood waiting to cash a check or has run his hands over the sleek fender of a new car. Roads, fences, tree trunks, stems, horizons, roofs, and marching soldiers all form lines.

Mood and action are often attributed to orientation and shape of lines. Vertical and horizontal lines are considered formal and stable, and oblique lines are said to be dynamic. Anybody who has ever slipped while in the vertical, plunged through the oblique, and come to rest in the horizontal can understand why vertical and horizontal are considered stable and oblique considered dynamic.

S-shaped lines are said to be tranquil. An s-shaped road may appear tranquil, but how many people would find tranquility in an s-coiled snake? The ultimate effect of lines, or any element, depends on subject matter and treatment.

Interestingly enough, the appeal of lines has a physiological basis as the eye and brain seek them out as the basic building blocks in identifying objects. Certain cells in the visual cortex of the brain and neural pathways leading to it respond only to impulses from the retina that indicate certain line orientations. Other cells respond only to contour lines such as those formed by the outline of your hand when placed on a blue notebook. The value of responding to specific line orientations is that the brain can readily pick out edges, contours, and angles that indicate the end of one object or feature and the beginning of another. In other words, you can tell where your leg stops and your shoe starts.

Hard and angular, straight lines tend to be more active when oblique as in the colorful paint brush handles and to be more passive when horizontal or vertical as in the tree trunks below.

A taut rope and a sinewy arm, the texture of both clearly revealed, form lines of tension.

A meandering highway seems relaxed when compared with the tension of the straight lines in the other pictures on this spread.

SHAPE

When a line closes it forms an outline we call shape. Shape is two-dimensional. It shows only the horizontal and vertical dimensions and excludes depth or volume. Sought by the eye, shape quickly identifies many objects. Given even a partial outline of a cat, a house, or a face, you'll readily identify those things. Given just the color, texture, or a few lines from those same things, you'd have a more difficult time recognizing them.

For most objects, your mind holds one, perhaps two shapes as representative. However, not all objects can be whittled down to one shape, and the several other shapes of objects seen from different viewpoints can be mysterious abstractions.

For example, your hand takes many shapes with varying viewpoints. When you view the back of your hand with the fingers splayed, there's no doubt your hand is a hand. But if you hold your hand perpendicular to the

ground as if in prayer and look down at it, you see only the fingertips. And by holding the palm perpendicular to the ground and viewing it from the side, you see another "unhandlike" shape.

The purest of shapes is a silhouette. A silhouette strips away all hints of texture, form, and color, leaving a bare-bone shape that rouses the imagination to wonder what's not showing. In a sense, silhouettes appeal personally because the viewers

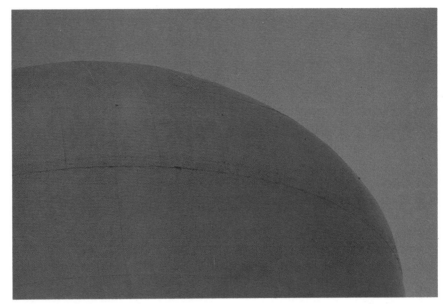

*Shapes appeal to the eye, whether they are varied and formed by a silhouette, **left,** or simple and merging in a wash of blue, **above,** a few and well-defined by frontlight, **below.***

Like most things, a hand, perhaps the most familiar of shapes, can show some unusual shapes if one takes the time to look for them.

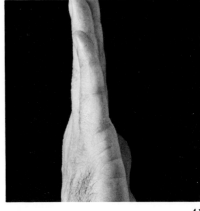

draw heavily on their own experiences to fill in the details. A silhouette might be compared to a radio story in which the listener hears only a sneering voice and pleading cries, and must fill in the handlebar mustache, the beady eyes, and the hook nose belonging to the thug lurking in our minds.

Shapes come to the fore most readily when an object is clearly separated from the background, either by tonal or color contrast, and when viewed from head-on. Color contrasts also call attention to shape because contours become obvious. Lipstick may be the most obvious use of color to highlight shape.

41

FORM

Form reveals the world in its three dimensions, adding volume and depth to the height and width of shape. Whereas shape identifies lips, form conveys their fullness. By rendering the form of a pear, a face, or any other subject, you portray it with a compelling realism that almost convinces the viewer to reach out and bite the pear.

Different forms arouse different responses. Forms of commonly held small objects like a wedge of cake or a bar of soap generally elicit a stronger physical response than forms of large objects, like houses, that can only be viewed. Gentle, curving forms sugges-tive of the human body often arouse pleasant and sensual feelings. Hard, angular forms, like staircases, atypical of nature, provoke more analytical, perhaps even aggressive feelings.

Showing volume and depth of form on a flat piece of paper seems illogical until you consider that vision itself senses depth and volume from the comparatively flat surface of the retina. Although the eyes gather from a scene stereoscopic and other cues not in a photograph, the most important cue in conveying form is readily depicted photographically. That cue is shading. And the key to shading is lighting. By choosing lighting that clearly differentiates the varying surfaces of a subject with highlights and shadows, you have delineated form—nostrils swell, eye sockets recede, biceps bulge.

Varying degrees of harsh and diffuse sidelighting best reveal form, the most suitable combination depending on subject matter and intent. A diffuse sidelight, such as from a northern window, yields a wide tonal range. The gradual transition from highlight to dark shadow easily accents subtle forms, such as the striations of a stomach or the ridges of tendons on the back of a hand. Diffuse directional light also works well in showing the form of curved subjects like pears and tree limbs. Harsh sidelight, such as that of an electronic flash or the sun, gives more contrast, abruptly shifting from highlight to shadow. It may hide small details in shadow.

Thomas Cobb

In all three pictures, form is strongly defined by sidelighting. With the third dimension of form revealed, each photograph comes closest to imitating the depth that is part of reality. The ability of KODAK TRI-X Pan Film to yield fine tonal gradation helps bring out the form in the black-and-white photograph.

TEXTURE

A cousin to form, texture describes the three dimensions of a surface and is commonly described as smooth or rough. Just as highlighting form gives an immediacy to a subject so does highlighting texture. The subject becomes real.

Texture beckons with a waggle and a caress. The waggle appeals to sight. The caress to touch. Perceiving texture in a photograph is like trying to comfort a scolded child. Standoffish, sulking, the child keeps her distance, letting you see but not touch her. You want to reach out and soothe her so badly that you can feel her in your arms though she isn't there. So it is with texture. You see it so clearly you think you can feel it, though you can't.

Sight is aloof, out there, away from us. Touch is intimate, here, next to us. Touch is the clothes on our back, the coins spilling from our hands. Texture is touch. In a photograph, texture evokes a variety of sensations and feelings associated with touching that texture. When you bite into an apple, the tongue not only feels its texture but reports on its tangy taste, and the nose notes its aroma. When you walk across the beach on a summer day, the feet feel not only the grit of the sand but leap from stabs of heat. Hot, cold, sweet, slippery, sticky, sharp, dull, and other sensations pal around with texture.

Small by nature, texture easily eludes our notice. Learn to think of textures in different ways. Oranges and eggs are relatively smooth. But relative is relative. Enlarge an orange to the size of the earth and its crevices swallow the Grand Canyon.

Delicate textures like an orange peel are best defined by a harsh, skimming sidelight. Large, rough textures like oak bark are best revealed by diffuse light from the side or front. On rough textured objects, a harsh, skimming sidelight may throw shadows that hide detail.

©J. Peter Mortimer

Textures abound in this picture. The knap of the blanket, the peeling wall, the saddle, the hands and face, even the leg of the bunk bed, all combine to make a vivid portrait of the spartan life of a cowboy.

*Head-on lighting, **bottom picture**, diminishes texture whereas oblique lighting, **top picture**, enhances texture.*

The two sides of a sand dune reveal the effect of lighting on texture. The smoothness of the left side of the dune is further stressed by head-on lighting which suppresses texture. The ripples on the right side of the dune are accentuated by oblique lighting.

Kathleen Norris Cook

We tend to think of texture as small but in a photograph large becomes small and a plowed field can exhibit texture.

Anselm Spring

Michael Melford

By using three distinct blocks of color, the photographer unifies the photograph.

COLOR

"Give them any color they want so long as it's black." Attributed to Henry Ford talking about his Model T's, those sentiments have fallen by the wayside. A more accurate, if not more recent, assessment of the power of color was made by Eric the Red who discovered a barren land and tried to lure settlers by dubbing it Greenland.

Powers to affect mind and body have long been attributed to color. Red excites. Blue calms. Green heals. Brown saddens.

The most obvious power of color is that of attraction. Throughout evolution, barter between bright colors and the eye has built a strong relationship. Dandelions and roses have used bright color to indicate a willingness to trade meals for a delivery of pollen. Apples and strawberries have used bright color to indicate a willingness to trade meals for a spreading of seed. Humans have used bright colors for everything imaginable, from hawking shampoo to peddling pens.

Although the appeal of bright colors is natural, subtle colors shouldn't be overlooked. How often do you use subtle colors in your photographs? Probably not too often. Dull is dull. Or is it? Look again. Observe and analyze. Dwell within the somber browns of November corn stubble. Daydream in the pastel greens of spring buds. Contemplative. Melancholic. Introspective. Only thoughtless photographers are dull.

Bold and Bright Colors

They razzle. They dazzle. They sizzle and tussle. If they aren't the intended subject, bold and bright colors soon will be, overthrowing form, deposing line, ousting texture. Recognize them as the sirens of photography trying to lure you onto the rocks.

Handled with care, bold and bright colors can spotlight, stimulate, and, surprisingly, sadden. If they are the subject, treat them simply. Take one or two colors and shape them into graphic designs by using viewpoint and framing to exclude the extraneous. More than two bold and bright colors tend to overwhelm and confuse, an effect useful only if you want to overwhelm and confuse.

If they are secondary to the subject, subordinate bold and bright hues. You can exclude them; you can remove them if portable, you can hide them in shadows, or you can use black-and-white film.

46

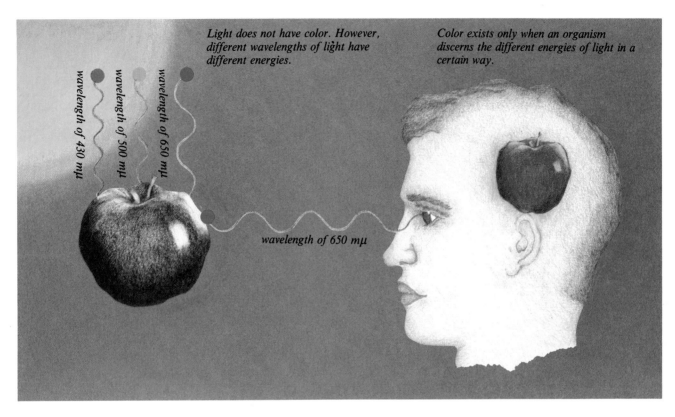

Light does not have color. However, different wavelengths of light have different energies.

Color exists only when an organism discerns the different energies of light in a certain way.

wavelength of 430 mμ

wavelength of 500 mμ

wavelength of 650 mμ

wavelength of 650 mμ

Vision and Color:

Apples, oranges, lemons, limes, daffodils, violets—the world drips with color so it might come as little surprise that we perceive it so well. Yet it should be a surprise. Among the millions of living creatures only a handful—some apes, birds, a few fish and insects—can distinguish color.

Although light itself is colorless, color has it roots in light. Light possesses not color but different energies corresponding to the different wavelengths of light. It is the way that an organism interprets the energies of light that can give rise to the perception of color. Even so, the mere capability of responding to different energies of light doesn't automatically grant perception of color. Squirrels, alligators, and many other animals have the biological sophistication to distinguish different energies of light, but they lack the means to see it as color. Instead they see it in shades of grey, like a black-and-white photograph.

Only when the necessary biological sensor exists can color exist. That sensor is called a cone. Some seven million cones line the human retina. Cones consist of three types. Each type has a slightly different pigment molecule that is most sensitive to certain wavelengths of light. One type responds mostly to long wavelengths (usually seen as red), another to short wavelengths (usually seen as blue),and the last to intermediate wavelengths (usually seen as green). From mixtures of these three colors arise all colors. Thus if the red-perceiving cones are stimulated, we see red. If the red- and blue-perceiving cones are stimulated, we see magenta. If the red- and green-perceiving cones are stimulated, we see yellow. If all three types of cones are equally stimulated, we see shades of grey, depending upon how strong the stimulation is.

Because sunlight contains a full range of wavelengths that stimulates all three types of cones, it normally appears colorless. How then is it that your socks or car can appear red if they are lit by the neutral light of the sun? Because they absorb some wavelengths and reflect others. We see the ones they reflect. For example, your red socks appear red, because they reflect the wavelengths that stimulate the red receptors and absorb the wavelengths that would have stimulated the other receptors. Which wavelengths of light an object absorbs or reflects depends on its atomic and molecular structure.

A small spot of bright color in an area of neutral color immediately attracts the eye, highlighting the subject.

*Whether color is muted by twilight, **top**, or fog, **bottom**, the effect results in the same moodiness.*

MUTED COLORS

Muted colors work because they suggest—and indeed often derive from—moody weather and moody times of day. What weather mutes color? Fog, rain, snow. Now think of your experiences and associations with such weather: the blare of foghorns, the sweep of windshield wipers, the slants of snow against headlights. It's a time to retreat indoors to a book or a nap, occasionally arising to part the curtains and gaze outside. Somber, quiet, melancholic, whatever feelings you associate with such weather will surface in your photographs of muted colors.

Much of the mood derives from the low level of illumination and the low contrast of such times. With slide film, camera exposure affects apparent illumination. You can make a scene appear darker and more dismal by underexposing slide film or more cheerful by overexposing it. If the contrast is too low for your purposes and you are using KODAK EKTACHROME Film, you can increase the contrast by doubling the film speed (do it for the whole roll and request push processing from your dealer). You also increase the grain slightly, an effect that may intensify moodiness.

In bad weather and at dusk, photographers all too often head indoors. Don't. Dress appropriately, protect your camera by slipping it under your coat or into a plastic bag with a hole cut out for the lens, and venture outdoors. You can make rain and snow show as blurred strings by using shutter speeds around 1/30 second. You can freeze them with electronic flash or a shutter speed of 1/125 second or faster. For rain or snow to show, it must contrast with the background, so include a dark background in part of your picture.

HARMONIC COLORS

Harmonic colors are similar colors, and as the word harmonic suggests, a group of similar colors tends to be agreeable and pleasant. Oranges and reds, blues and violets, greens and limes are harmonic combinations. Although easily found, many people overlook harmonic colors because of their quietness.

They are especially prevalent in nature—the quiet browns of a field in November, the gentle greens of the same field in May. When photographing outdoors, look for harmonic colors and use them to instill a pensive mood to your photographs.

Harmonic colors unify a picture. Dissimilar subjects become rooted in the firmament of color.

Sometimes you can induce or strengthen harmonic colors through the use of subtle filtration. Made of gelatin, KODAK Color Compensating Filters are available in red, green, blue, yellow, cyan, and magenta. They are made in several densities from a wisp of color to medium-dark color. Using filtration to create a harmonic color effect works best in diffuse lighting and when the scene has many neutral or near-neutral colors that will pick up the filter color. Strong lighting and strong colors muscle out subtle filtration.

Eric Albrecht, by permission of Horticulture. © 1983

Harmonic colors link together the various elements of a photograph. Blue links the chair to the flowers, even to the magenta flowers which show some bluishness. The empty chair also evokes thoughts of the person who sometimes sits there admiring the flowers.

SIZE

Every object has size. A screwdriver has size, a snowmobile has size. But a subject's size isn't automatically conveyed by a photograph. If size is important, and often it is, then you need to consider how to convey your impressions of size.

First of all, whatever a subject's size, big as an elephant or small as a pea, it can be rendered no larger than the film frame or the enlarged photograph. For most, but not all things you photograph, this means the image size will be less than the real size.

How much of the photograph the subject fills contributes to impressions of its size. You can make large subjects seem small by giving them but a small portion of the picture area. A picture of an oak taking up only a fraction of the picture area makes the oak seem but a small part of a vast expanse. By filling the frame with the oak, it now seems considerably larger.

Filling the frame also changes the emphasis of the picture. Before, the picture was of a small subject in a large space, now it is a picture of a tree—the weaving of its limbs, the texture of its bark.

To stress the largeness of large things or the smallness of small things, or to invert and make large seem small and small seem large, the subject must be counterpointed with a subject of known size. You must establish scale. A poodle atop an elephant, a bee atop an apple, a blueberry beneath a fork, a mountain climber atop a ridge—all of known size, all help create scale, give a sense of sizes.

By including a subject of known size, such as a car, the vastness of the landscape is revealed. Vastness is further emphasized by the strong perspective cues of the road and furrows vanishing into the distance.

Bruce Barnbaum

If the picture holds no obvious cues to size, small can seem large and large can seem small. What appears to be canyons of ice is actually a watermelt only a few feet high.

VISION AND SIZE:

Many beginning photographers have been disappointed when the mountain or horse that loomed so large when being photographed shows up so small in the picture. This is one instance where the physiology of seeing can mislead the photographer. Although the eye and camera form comparable images on the retina and the film, the brain adjusts the retinal image. This adjustment is called size constancy.

Optically, image size doubles with each halving of distance. For instance, the retinal image of a six-foot man standing ten feet away is twice the size of the retinal image when the man stands twenty feet away. At each distance, though, we see a six-foot man because the brain adjusts the physical image on the retina to give us a fairly constant mental image. Try this. With both eyes open, hold one hand at arm's length and the other at half arm's length. Even though the farther hand forms a retinal image half the size of the nearer hand, both hands appear to be roughly the same size.

Even when retinal images of the same size are formed, the brain quickly recognizes the objects may be of different size. For instance, an apple in your hand and a car in the neighbor's driveway may form equal-size retinal images. Do you perceive these objects as being the same size? Of course not. By experience you know they're different sizes. Illusionists sometimes play on the brain's influence over size perception by using miniature or oversize chairs to alter one's sense of spatial relationships. We expect chairs to be of a certain size in relation to ourselves, and arrange spatial relationships around that size.

DEPTH

The first two dimensions are height and width. The third is depth. In an object, depth is called form. But here we are concerned with the depth of an overall scene. The more three dimensional a photographic scene appears, the more real it seems. Soon you forget you are holding a photograph and feel as if you have become part of the scene. Sometimes, however, you may want to suppress reality, you may want a scene to appear flat. And you'll be able to do that as well once you understand what makes a scene appear three dimensional. (The visual cues to depth are discussed on pages 54-55.)

In creating three dimensionality, depth need not mean great distance. A desk top can appear as three dimensional as an air field--if its depth is made obvious. Depth is stressed when cues in the scene make the viewer aware that objects are in the foreground, midground, or background, and that they are separated by space. The stronger these cues, the stronger the sense of depth.

Several depth cues arise only when objects exist both in the foreground and background, or midground. A lone fork lying left to right in a sink will give little sense of depth. But place a sponge a few inches behind the fork and the sense of depth increases. Now there is a foreground subject and a background subject, and the space between them. The fork may overlap part of the sponge to signify it's in front of the sponge and their apparent sizes can be compared, indicating how far apart they are.

Spaces between and around objects are important. By buffering an object with space, you announce it has volume, that it exists apart and at some distance from other objects. And by composing the photo so that there are spaces between ob-jects, you let the eye roam from foreground to midground and squeeze into the background. You make the eye notice that there are different areas of midground, different areas of background, and that these areas recede. You give the picture depth.

These two pictures use different cues (p. 54-55) to reveal depth. In the photo below, shadowing creates strong forms. Overlapping objects make us aware that one thing is in front of another. Subject placement points out the foreground, midground, and background, and leaves some open spaces for the eye to travel to these areas. The photo opposite displays classic depth by giving an immediate sense of distance. By shooting from a low angle, the photographer creates upward dislocation of the eye. He also exaggerates the textural gradient cue by including cobblestones in the immediate foreground.

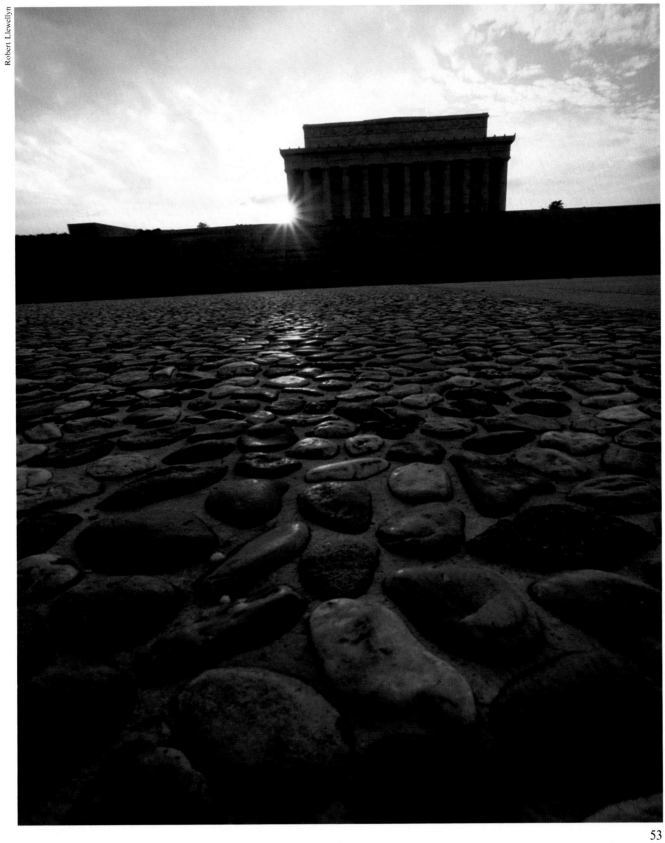

In photography, the ultimate way of creating three-dimensionality is through stereoscopy—the practice of using a camera with two lenses to create two pictures of the same subject but with slightly different views. When a person looks at those two different views in a stereoscope, they form one three-dimensional image— just as the brain does with the two views provided by the eyes.

Fortunately, there are other ways to create a sense of three-dimensionality using normal photographic practices. The mind uses several one-eyed cues to perceive depth and distance. By making use of the following one-eyed (monocular) cues, you can heighten the illusion of depth in your photographs. These cues are as follows:

1. Linear perspective
2. Aerial perspective
3. Size diminuition
4. Texture gradient
5. Overlap
6. Shadowing
7. Upward dislocation

LINEAR PERSPECTIVE
Perhaps the most powerful and most often used cue to gauge distance is linear perspective. Linear perspective is simply the convergence of receding parallel lines and planes. Railroad tracks, roads, and skyscrapers show linear perspective. You can exaggerate linear perspective by using a wide-angle lens and including foreground lines as well as background lines.

TEXTURE GRADIENT
A texture gradient is a form of size diminution. With distance, texture becomes smaller and denser. The mind recognizes this feature and uses it as a cue for perceiving distance. On this rocky beach, the stones are of similar size. The smaller and more tightly packed they appear, the more distant you perceive them to be. They form a texture gradient.

AERIAL PERSPECTIVE
Aerial perspective refers to how the atmosphere alters the appearance of light. As distance increases, the atmosphere scatters more light, causing subjects to look increasingly paler, less sharp, and to have lower contrast. Distant subjects may look somewhat bluer or yellower. The effect is most noticeable on landscapes over several miles but may be noticeable in hazy urban areas. With black-and-white film, you can increase the effect by using a blue filter and reduce it with a polarizing filter, or a deep yellow, orange, or red filter. With color film, you can reduce the haze effect by using a polarizing filter.

UPWARD DISLOCATION
Upward dislocation simply means that subjects that are farther away are usually higher in the visual field. By showing a subject high within a photograph, you give the viewer an additional cue that the subject is farther away. For example, the distance to a boat a hundred yards away is stressed more by placing the boat high within the photograph than by placing it low. You can exaggerate the effect of upward dislocation by using a low viewpoint and including the foreground.

OVERLAP

A subject that overlaps another subject appears to be in front of the farther subject. An apple overlapping an orange obviously fronts the orange.

Not a particularly strong cue in emphasizing distance, overlap can work well with other cues, such as size diminution. The old framing trick in which a photographer includes a foreground frame of leaves or branches stresses distance by combining an overlap cue with size diminution.

SIZE DIMINUITION

Size diminuition means that the more distant a subject is, the smaller it appears. It is thus related to linear perspective. From experience, the mind knows that certain things, such as people and boats, have certain sizes. If they appear quite small, then it is because they are quite far away, or so the mind reasons. In photographs, distance can be stressed by including a foreground subject of known size as well as a background subject.

SHADOWING

In the discussion of form and texture, we have seen how shadowing can heighten three-dimensionality by making forms and textures apparent. Similarly, in stressing distance and depth, shadowing works by making forms apparent and by creating space between them. Again backlighting and sidelighting work best since they cast shadows seen by the camera. Shadowing can also indicate or exaggerate the size of things. Shadows on the ground or background can show aspects of form not shown by the objects themselves.

VISION AND DEPTH PERCEPTION:

Day in and day out, the mind builds a three-dimensional world from two-dimensional and even nondimensional data. The eye muscles provide nondimensional data. As an object comes closer, the eye muscles rotate the eyes inward to track the object. This inward tracking is called convergence. The greater the angle of convergence of the eyes, the greater the muscle strain. The degree of muscle strain indicates the angle of convergence, which the brain converts into an indication of subject distance.

Much of our success in depth perception results from using two eyes set 2 1/2 inches apart in the head that provide slightly different views of a subject. The brain combines these different views to form one three-dimensional image. In combining the different views, the brain sorts the differences between them and converts the differences into cues of three-dimensionality. Like hands scooping a slice of snow and molding it into a snowball, the brain rounds out things. For example, hold your left hand edgewise and vertically a foot in front of your face. Look at it with the right eye closed, then with the left eye closed. With only the right eye open, you see some of the palm of the hand and little of the back. With only the left eye open, you see much of the back of the hand but little of the palm. With both eyes open, you see the palm and the back of the hand as the brain combines the two images to round out your hand.

Combining two different images to create three-dimensionality is called stereoscopy.

VISION AND PERSPECTIVE

Works of art did not reveal perspective until 15th Century Renaissance artists devised rules for rendering perspective. By our standards of perspective, ancient Chinese and Egyptian paintings seemed flat.

Although western civilization abounds with right angles and straight lines, the ingredients important to perceiving perspective, we do not see perspective in its full effect. The problem is not with the eye since images formed on the retina show perspective. However, the brain adjusts the retinal image, usually reducing apparent perspective. Thus, when we look up at a skyscraper it does not seem to tip backwards, nor do its edges drastically converge, though both things happen on the retina and on film. However, we fully recognize depth as conveyed by perspective in photographs.

In Africa, the Zulus live in round huts and have few possessions with right angles or straight lines. Their world is almost devoid of linear perspective cues. Not surprisingly, they have a poorly developed sense of linear perspective. As much was indicated by a series of perspective tests, such as the line-length illusion shown below, which showed the Zulus seldom saw perspective illusions as did people of western civilization.

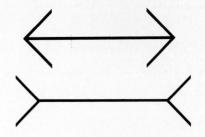

Looking

The more you look, the more you find.

Photographs like these (below and opposite) require two things of the photographer: searching and recognition.

To see a scene you might think you need only look at it. But it's not that simple. One scene can be viewed in many ways, and if you look at it in only one way, you miss a great deal. By developing and refining the ways you look at a scene, you can increase your perceptiveness and the number of photographs you take.

You might compare how you look at a scene with how a calculator functions. Let's say the chairs, rocks, windows—the basic units of a scene—are numbers. If you see them in only one way, you function only in the add mode. But if you see them in several ways, you function like an advanced calculator. You add, subtract, divide, multiply, and perform trigonometric functions. Faced with the same basic units, you can do much more with them if you vary your way of seeing.

As mentioned earlier in the book, the human eye tends to fixate on individual objects—the tree, the rock, the car, the building. Overcome this tendency to see only individual objects. See not only the objects, but the relationships. Look at parts of objects, at relationships between parts of objects. Although you cannot look near and far simultaneously, the camera can. Examine how a daisy in the foreground links to the boat in the background. See how changing the viewpoint changes relative positions of the daisy and the boat. Look at things near, things far, things up and down.

Given the number of things out there and the number of ways they can be looked at, careful seeing can be tiring. But it's also rewarding. You'll come to appreciate the beauty of things previously overlooked and wonder at the new relationships you uncover.

A camera licenses you to observe and delight in the world. Use that license. If you have not yet found any joy in photography, it is because you have yet to see and appreciate. If you have lost that joy, it is because you have let picture-taking usurp seeing. Keep first things first, and you will enjoy photography. If a photograph does not capture the emotion or beauty you felt, instead of despairing, count yourself lucky for the original feeling and the memory of it.

Feeling good about photography, being relaxed in observing the world will help you feel good about yourself and ultimately help you take better pictures.

Robert Llewellyn

Pete Turner/The Image Bank

FINDING PICTURES

Although varying your way of viewing is important, it is not the most important part of seeing. The most important part of seeing, perhaps the most important part of photography—a part much unappreciated, seldom mentioned, and greatly underrated—is the art of searching. Photographs don't just happen. The photographer must find them, must make them, must have camera in hand and be looking.

Look at this much-published Pete Turner photograph. It's a remarkable photograph, not only for its simplicity, which is powerful; not only for its mood, which is strong; not only for its design, which is compelling; but also for what it doesn't show—the photographer at the scene. Turner was there. That's why he got the picture. Buy the fanciest camera, read the best books, hone the sharpest eye, and all

will be for naught if you aren't there to use them.

Once there, what are you looking for? What is the Holy Grail for which you search? It is something different, something unusual, something to catch the viewer's eye.

But different and unusual are vague. What things are different and unusual? Different and unusual need not be belly dancers or pearl divers or other exotic subjects. Common and usual subjects can make different and unusual photographs. Photographers prove this time and again.

What then is different and unusual? The things we discuss in this book. The lines of leaf edges, the form of a soap dish, the texture of a swan's back, the forms and colors in a new housing tract. They are the echoing juxtaposition of two feet and two leaves on a porch. They are the overwhelming detail in a boy's face, they

are the frieze of arms and legs projecting from bathing-suited torsos. They are everything out there—found and photographed in a way that entertains the eye.

Once there, wherever "there" may be, should you look for a specific subject like driftwood or galloping horses? Or should you lift the sashes of your mind and let fly in what may? Here's what Jay Maisel, one of America's leading photographers, recommends: "I think the most dangerous thing a photographer can do is go out with a picture already in his mind's eye. While you're thinking about what you want to happen you're very likely missing what is happening."

Pete Turner says, "Have a subject in mind, even if it's as general as a beach or trees, and work with that...the person very well might come upon something totally unexpected." Are they giving conflicting

Mary Matsumoto

Wind blowing through hair, idle chatter of small children, evening sun bathing faces, the pull of gravity and centrifugal force as the swings arc into the sky—this picture engages many pleasant feelings by conjuring up sensations we have felt under similar circumstances.

advice? Not really. Each is saying, above all, to keep an open mind when photographing.

IGNORING YOUR OTHER SENSES

All too frequently a photograph doesn't agree with your memory of a scene. Though you poke and prod, the photograph remains lifeless, a corpse mocking the vividness of what you felt, of what you thought you saw. Your first reaction: disbelief. Something went wrong because "I know what I saw and this isn't what I saw." The camera screwed up. Second reaction: disappointment. "Why didn't I capture the scene as I saw it? How can I avoid this in the future?"

The problem is not with how you see, but with how you react. When you see to photograph a scene, you also hear, smell, feel, and taste that scene, and you react to all those senses. But you can't smell, hear, taste, or feel a photograph, at least

not as you did in the original scene. You can only see it. You can only react to the visual elements.

Photographing a waterfall on a sunny spring day, you hear the roar of the waterfall, the gurgling of the stream, the chirping of the birds, the rustling of branches. You feel the warmth of the sun, the cool of the shade, the wet of the spray. And though you see and intend to photograph the waterfall, you also see the deer retreating into the woods, the leaves dancing in the sun, the trout gliding in the pool, and many other things not to be included in the photograph. And your mind joins the dance, rejoicing at the end of winter, the start of spring, the renewal of life.

The chirping, the gurgling, the fragrances, the sights, all combine to form an impression of the scene much greater than that conveyed by the photograph. The photograph is but a

piece of paper. Chirpless and odorless, it is outnumbered by your original sensations.

If you want a photograph to represent your impression of a scene, you must first obtain an accurate visual impression. As you look into the viewfinder, filter out the chirps and fragrances, suppress extraneous associations floating through your mind. Concentrate on the visual elements within the viewfinder and pan out the visual nuggets to be melted down and cast into a photograph.

Are the visual elements strong? Do they match your impressions of the scene? Can they be manipulated? Should you include more or exclude more? What should you emphasize? What should you subordinate? Once you are able to isolate and analyze the visual elements in a scene, you'll find your photographs agreeing with your original impressions.

FRAGMENTS

When you look at a scene, you can see a subject as a part of the scene or a part of a subject in the scene. For the next few pages, we consider the effects of varying vision from a fragment of a subject, to the whole subject in its context, to contriving strange relationships.

Each of us is well versed in photographing whole things, but we may not be so well versed in photographing parts of things. Review your work and see if you sometimes photograph parts of things. Easily photographed, parts of things may not be so easily seen because of our emphasis on the whole. Normally we see whole things and combine the whole things into an impression of what's before us. Force yourself to ignore the whole and look at parts. This feat is more easily accomplished by looking through the camera viewfinder to keep your eye from wandering.

Once aware of the power of parts, you'll find them easily. Parts are graphic. Not showing the whole subject shifts from the information and emotion associated with the whole, be it an apple or a lobster boat, to something more abstract. That something may be a design of color, line, form, or shape. It may be a mood of warmth or melancholy. It may even be an intellectual exercise, a visual riddle or pun. Fragmented relationships often leave gaps that challenge the viewer to fill in the missing pieces according to the viewer's psyche. When pictures aren't literal, they invite many interpretations.

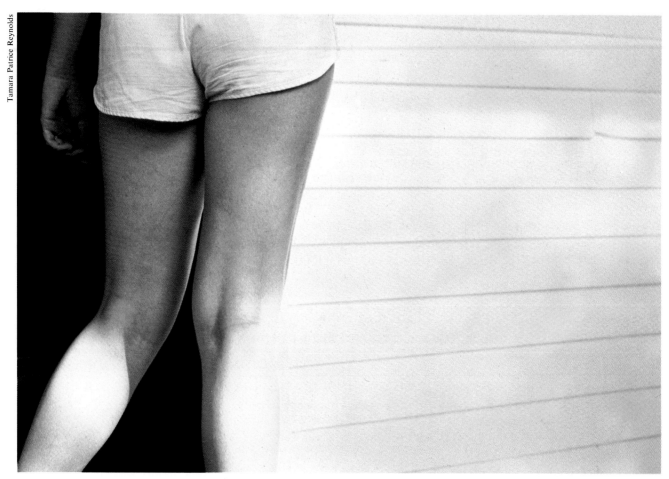

Tamara Patrice Reynolds

THE WHOLE

Showing a whole subject in a photograph parallels our most natural way of seeing. The reason we like to see whole things is simple: we are trying to make sense of what we see. It is easier to make sense of things if you see all of them than if you see part of them.

Filling the picture with a subject both simplifies and complicates. It simplifies by sending the supporting cast offstage where you don't have to worry about directing them. And when you have but one dominant subject, viewers don't wonder what they're supposed to see. There's only one thing they can see. That's simple.

That's also complicated. The subject—be it a Bentwood Rocker, a jetty, a thunderhead—standing by itself, center stage, up front, with eyes riveted to it, must soliloquize. Alone, it must implore. Alone, it must cajole. Alone, it must persuade. Alone, it must convince you, the viewer, that it is worth admiring or hating but, above all, worth your time. Not all subjects can stand alone before a critical audience. And though the subject may be alone, you still must worry about composition, lighting, viewpoint, and the other details that enter into making any picture.

Showing detail is often important when filling the frame with the subject. To capture the most detail, use a fine-grained film such as KODACOLOR VR 100, KODAK EKTACHROME 100, or KODAK Technical Pan (black-and-white) Film.

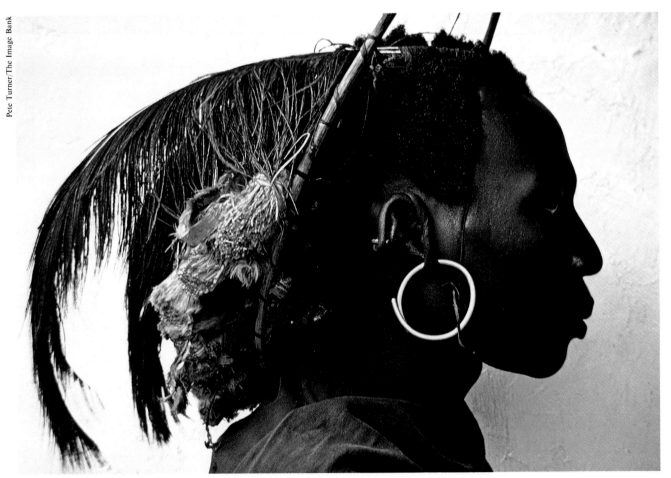

Pete Turner/The Image Bank

IN CONTEXT

A cherry tree in bloom. A cherry tree in bloom in an orchard. A cherry tree in bloom in front of a split-level house. A cherry tree in bloom in a parking lot. A cherry tree in bloom.

Everything is somewhere. Often you can better reveal the nature of a subject by showing where it is.

The most straightforward approach is to show a subject in its expected context—a wildflower on a forest floor, a sailboat bobbing near a lighthouse. Although incidental or obvious relationships like these may explain, may even excite, they do little to reform thoughts about the subject. People expect a boat to be near a lighthouse, so there it is.

Other times we may expect to see a subject such as a lighthouse in a certain context and be surprised to see it in a fresh context. Surprise delights the viewer and rewards him for looking.

However, when people don't know what to expect, surroundings can reinforce a feeling, add atmosphere, or create a new feeling about the subject. For instance, a head-and-shoulders portrait of a woman may say something completely different from a photograph showing the woman relaxing in her opulent "green" room.

The immediate problem of picturing a subject in context is handling the increase in objects included in the picture. Instead of handling one, you're juggling three, four, or five subjects which, if not cleanly handled, thud to the ground. Success usually comes from good choice of viewpoint and composition. Explore them carefully. Be sure that the overall effect conforms with your intentions and precisely states your case.

A lighthouse, one of the most commonly photographed subjects, is seen here in a different way. How often have you seen the landed side of a lighthouse photographed? A dirt road and a telephone booth, a more modern sort of sentinel, seem to poke fun of our romantic images of lighthouses.

Len Jenshel

STRANGE RELATIONS

For more provocative images, look for or create unexpected relationships. They work like word associations. You say "hot," expect to hear "cold," and do a double-take when the response is "banana." Hot—banana? Within any given scene you can relate photographic bananas to monkeys, moons, or mothers by adjusting your viewpoint and framing to include different things. A face next to a doorknob. A doorknob next to a clock. A doorknob next to a slipper.

In reality, the doorknob may be several feet from the clock or slipper and have no apparent relationship until you show them side-by-side in a photograph. The combinations are endless and you can add items like your hand, your leg, a bottle, or anything else that strengthens your visual statement. Commercial photographers excel in grabbing attention with unexpected relationships, such as a blood-filled syringe plunged into a tomato.

Just as you can have differences in kinds of subjects, so can you have differences in their qualities such as texture, color, size, shape, and brightness. You can counterpoint rough with smooth, light with dark. You can work straight against curved, small against large.

Above, *two feet, two leaves, each side by side. The eye bounces from feet to leaves and back again, noting similarities in size, texture, form, and arrangement.*

A disembodied doll's face imprisoned by a mirror angled in one direction; a woman and her shadow frozen in a mirror angled in another direction. What is their relationship? What is the woman holding in her hands? The clues held back and a scene revealed only in reflections disorient and frustrate us.

© Tom Benson

Frank Revi

VIEWPOINT

The place from which you see or photograph the subject is the viewpoint. Viewpoint can do two things. It can show the subject from an unusual angle to reveal a side seldom seen. It can organize the physical relationships between subjects.

No doubt you know that you can photograph a subject from above, from below, from the front, the back, the side, and a variety of other positions. But knowing isn't doing. Do you exploit viewpoint? Do you examine a subject from all angles, looking for both the side seldom seen and the viewpoint that organizes the scene?

Facing forward, some four to six feet above the ground, the eyes of the human skim over what's under them and skim under what's over them. Of-

ten photographers become lazy and take most of their pictures while standing and looking straight ahead.

Common and conventional, the upright view can become boring. You can't afford to bore. Flex your knees as well as your mind. Climb and see as the giraffe. Stoop and see as the mouse.

Nose to the ground, observe the mountainous range of roots, the glaring eyes of hubcaps, the muzzle of the sleeping dog, the jungle of grass. Watch the blossoms sway overhead, leap aside when walnuts crash, shudder at the whooshing roars from the asphalt plains. With the eyes of the mouse, perhaps you'll understand that the tulip previously at your feet stretches skyward to capture sunlight and flag down bees with its bright

banner of a blossom. Perhaps how you see the world depends on where you see it from.

From atop a picnic table or parking garage, look down and photograph. See how an aerial viewpoint flattens things, turns them into two-dimensional designs. Only by trying on several viewpoints can you find the one that fits.

When you spot a subject, you often see it from an accidental viewpoint, a viewpoint of chance that may or may not lead to the best photograph. You were walking by, looked to the left, said "Oh, I like that," pulled out your camera and photographed it. Fine. But don't rely solely on chance. Consider that the first and coincidental viewpoint may have been chosen not by the eyes of the photographer, but

Michael Melford

by the eyes of the everyday person.

The eyes of the everyday person like to identify things. They like characteristic shapes; they like revealing forms; they like key details. The eyes of the everyday person strive to recognize what they see and yield to the viewpoint giving recognition.

But will the everyday viewpoint give a good photograph? Instead of casually submitting to the viewpoint that identifies, compare it with viewpoints that contribute emotional and aesthetic characteristics also.

Be wary of shooting from an unusual viewpoint when the subject itself is remarkable. Instead of calling attention to the subject, you may call attention to the technique, to the fact that you were on the ground looking up when you took the picture.

*A high viewpoint, **left,** flattens things out, emphasizing shape and design. A low viewpoint, **above,** creates perspective distortion, making things converge vertically.*

Viewpoint makes the picture below work. Not only did the photographer find a view showing the relationship between fractured ice and skyscrapers, he also chose a low viewpoint so the ice fragments could be seen jutting skyward, mimicking the skyscrapers.

Art Walker

65

VIEWPOINT

Viewpoint organizes. And reorganizes. Arise from your chair and keeping your eye on the television, walk about. See how composition, spatial, and contextual relationships change. From one viewpoint, the coffee table is in front of the television; from another it is to the side of the television; from yet another it has slipped out of view. With each shift of viewpoint, shapes and forms change, objects emerge and disappear.

Shifts in viewpoint can dramatically alter the feel of a photograph. The change may occur because the scene is rearranged. It may also occur because the lighting direction changes. All the details of a frontlighted church vanish when you change your viewpoint so backlighting silhouettes the church.

Sometime, photograph from different viewpoints, purposefully trying to change the mood.

In these photographs of the church, composition, lighting, and weather all play important roles, but the most important role is that of viewpoint. Only from a hilltop viewpoint can the church and surrounding countryside be bathed by the light of sunrise. Only from within the adjoining cemetery can a newly dug grave be included to reveal the true purpose of church and cemetery. Only from across the road can a humorous "For Sale" sign, a beer bottle, some weeds, and a passing car be included to create a rather cluttered and disintegrating feeling. Viewpoint casts the mold in which the photograph is set.

Treating the subject

Listen. Hear the unspoken tale of the subject, a tale never before told. Listen. Hear the apple tell of budding growth beneath the spring sun, of sweet ripening, of the fall to ground, of the dissolution of flesh and the pride of rebirth. Hear the joy of the wave upon resurrection from ocean depths, hear it shout as it leaps into the sun and crashes swooshing across the sand, and hear it murmur in mourning as it withdraws. Listen to the subject, to yourself: then tell the story.

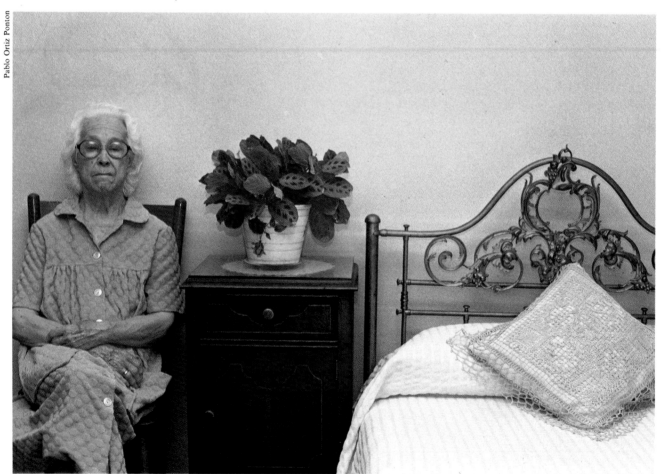

Pablo Ortiz Ponton

INTERPRETING

The undercurrent sweeping through this book has been that of interpretation. But when told to interpret, we react as if we have heard street directions and become more lost than before. The idea of interpretation, although it sounds good, seems vague and ill-fitting. Just how does one interpret?

Problems arise with interpretation because most of us have only a nodding acquaintance with the things we photograph. We know enough about trees, streams, and flowers to recognize and categorize them, but not so much as to be able to appreciate qualities unique to them. Nor do we know so little as to be awed and see them as wondrous. Let's face it, to most of us, trees are trees and streams are streams.

We also have but a nodding acquaintance with our feelings about what we're photographing. We haven't given much thought to what trees and cars mean to us. We have coexisted with them, that's all.

However, if we don't give them some thought, if we don't interpret, our photographs will be uninspiring. They will lack backbone. They'll be like any other car in the parking lot. Interpretation comes from the courage to learn your feelings and the courage to express them.

Only you can teach yourself how to interpret. It comes from inside. You're the only one that's been there.

Although it's easy to say that you can improve your photography by looking at subjects as if for the first time, following such advice is next to impossible. You can't simply banish past experiences.

Do just the opposite. Make an intense photographic study of a subject over a period of days, weeks, months, even years. Pick out a beach, a meadow, a room in the house, and explore the many ways you can photograph it. See how viewpoint, weather, surroundings, lighting, shutter speed, and the many other variables affect your interpretations.

Through an intense study not only will you discover new visual qualities in the subject but you will come to grip with your feelings about the subject. You will learn to interpret.

Michael Bishop often interprets the modern world with a grin. Here he plays several elements against each other, including symbols of different eras and a car parked at the edge of a desert which turns out to be a mural.

Left, *Stonehenge, mystical or mundane?
It all depends on your interpretation. By
silhouetting it against the evening sky and
including the full moon, Pete Turner
chose mystical. By showing a caretaker
mowing the lawn much as one mows a
front lawn, Arthur Meyerson opted for
the mundane view.*

*The grandeur of nature, a frequent theme
of photographers, is exemplified by
Sund's photograph of lightning striking
near Yosemite Falls and smiled at by
Minnick who shows Yosemite Falls in the
scarf of an admiring viewer.*

ASSOCIATIONS

The mind is a maker of analogies, a supplier of metaphors. It is a distributor of associations with a skull full of symbols waiting to be shipped out. Let a shoe into the mind and it's tacked to cobbler. Let in a cross and it's nailed to religion. Few objects entering the mind escape untouched.

Some objects like apples and roses and eagles have strong and traditional associations with temptation and love and strength. Other objects like shoes and avocados have weaker, less obvious associations. And associations even arise from nonobjects—from colors, from lighting. Green is healthful. Red is aggressive. Bright light energizes. Dim light dulls.

Associations ultimately depend on context. An apple on a teacher's desk means something different than an apple proffered by an alluring woman.

Associations can rouse strong emotions. The picture of the black child on this page may stir our sympathies. But its gut-wrenching power demonstrates the risks of association, for the only despair in this picture is that of our associations. Listen to the photographer who took the picture while in the Peace Corps:

> When my village mother worked in the fields, it was my responsibility to see that my village brother took his bath. I took him to the pond of rainwater that had collected behind the village and scrubbed him down once a day. He was so cute as he played in the water . . . and splashed around.

As a photographer, the associations you make with a scene may not be made by others. Consider the many associations a scene may elicit and work the one that best suits you.

Nearly every photograph arouses associations. Some, like the woman with the apple, stir rather definite associations. Others, like the snow fence, may not evoke any strong or definite associations.

Daniel J. Waite

Dan Neuberger

FAULTFINDING

Through observation and analysis, through heightened awareness, through inspiration and dogged searching, you found a subject. Now you're going to photograph it. Excited, elated, your spirits soar. Images dance in your mind. You can't wait to get back the pictures, though you have yet to take them.

Calm down. Don't let excitement carry you away. Would you want an excited surgeon cutting into you or an excited pilot landing your plane? No, you'd want a calm person capable of objective decision, a person sheltered from the storms of emotion, and it's that same person you want to take your photograph. Relax. How? By taking pictures. React and photograph your subject until the ripples of excitement abate and, when they do, begin photographing again. Or if you

want to conserve film, just observe until you can see the scene objectively and then begin photographing.

Emotion checked, excitement bottled, expectation corralled, now you can inspect the scene before you. Now you must nitpick. It's your last chance to get things right. Make sure your mind sees what the camera sees. React only to the visual elements in the viewfinder. As you look into the viewfinder, pretend you are standing in a friend's living room looking at a framed print taken by someone else. Viewpoint, subject position, depth of field, shutter speed, color balance, framing, lighting, composition. Check it all.

Now's the time to notice the distracting tree in the background and change your viewpoint.

Now's the time to spot the excessive contrast between the flare of sun-

light on the staircase and the shaded face in the window.

Now's the time to choose from among the many picture possibilities, the time to know that if you choose an unconventional treatment, you may shift emphasis from subject to technique. Nothing wrong with that if that's what you want. It's up to you.

In the moments between finding a subject and photographing it, you make many, perhaps hundreds, of decisions. Although you make these decisions almost automatically, periodically you should review your own decision-making process and see if it can be improved in any way. Listed below are some of the common decisions made. Glance at them—they may help—but above all, examine your own decision-making process, and see if too many things are decided by habit.

Equipment

Are you using an appropriate lens? Zoom lenses flare in backlighted scenes more than fixed-focal-length lenses. Telephoto lenses compress distances in scenes; wide-angles expand them. Is your film-speed dial set correctly? Are exposure compensation controls set correctly? Would a polarizing filter increase color saturation?

Without polarizing filter

With polarizing filter: richer colors

With a slight shift of viewpoint, the bridge tower is freed from merging with the building on its left.

For accurate tonal rendition of subjects with unusually high or low reflectance, you must adjust exposure when using a built-in camera meter. To make this white background appear white, the photographer increased exposure by 1 1/2 stops from the meter indication.

Without filter

With yellowish 81B filter

Color balance
With slide film especially, color casts may show if not corrected with filters. Cloudy days and open shade lend a slight bluishness to slides. You can eliminate the blue with an 81B filter. Subjects illuminated by a rising or setting sun may appear too yellow (although the yellowishness is usually considered pleasant). You can reduce or eliminate that yellow with an 82B filter. Unless seeking special effects, use daylight film in daylight and tungsten film in tungsten light.

Background
Inspect the background to make sure it doesn't distract. If you have a depth-of-field preview button, use it so that you can see how the background looks at the selected aperture. Do you want a sharp background because it adds to the feel of the picture? Or do you want it soft so the subject stands out?

Frame borders
Run your eye along the edges of the frame, checking to see that nothing is cut off that shouldn't be and that nothing is included that shouldn't be.

Composition
Examine the relationships between things in the scene. Check for awkward overlaps, disturbing spacing, and revealing organization. Is the emphasis in the proper place?

Exposure
Does the subject require any special exposure treatment as do brightly lit snow scenes, backlit scenes, and contrasty scenes? If shooting slides, would overexposure, which lightens colors, or underexposure, which saturates colors, be useful? Bracket when in doubt.

Depth of field
Is the depth of field enough? Too much? Use the depth-of-field scale on your camera or the depth-of-field preview button to check.

Check Lighting
Do shadows hide wanted detail? Can you lighten shadows with a reflector or flash? Does the angle of light suit the subject? If not, can you move to get a better angle without unduly upsetting composition?

Variations
If you really like the scene, shoot it from a number of viewpoints, using high and low angles, front and side positions. Shoot the scene in any way you can imagine.

GO WITH THE FLOW

Don't try to subdue a subject to your way of thinking—you can't push a piano through a porthole. Go with the flow. Be flexible. Adapt. The scene will not adapt to you, as you'll discover when viewing your pictures.

What's there is there. Work with it, not against it. If you had hoped to produce a glamorous portrait of the darling little girl next door but she's being an imp, adapt and capture the imp wrapping her pigtails around her face or giggling at your solemnity.

Don't let your expectations project mirages that leave you thirsting. Release expectations. Defy assumptions. Unite with the scene to see not what you want to see, but what's there. Then strengthen the strong points to build the photograph you want.

Sometimes a situation will prove to be unphotogenic. Recognize when that happens and be on your merry way looking for something else.

SIMPLIFY AND CLARIFY

When you take a photograph, you mean that photograph to show or say something, but sometimes your intent is obscure.

Obscurity arises from two common causes: Uncertainty of intent. Inclusion of too much. The solution? Be sure of your intent. Don't include too much.

Once you decide on intent, include only those things that contribute. Everything that doesn't contribute, detracts. Everything that doesn't add, subtracts. You want your viewers to notice the lines formed by a rowboat and its oars, but how can they when the rowboat and oars are seen amidst lilies, canoes, water-skiers, and picnickers?

Heed advice from another communicator, writer William Zinsser. "Writing improves in direct ratio to the number of things we can keep out of it that shouldn't be there." Substitute photography for writing and you have choice advice. In his book *On Writing Well*, Zinsser notes that clarity often suffers because the writer (in our case the photographer) holds too dear the attic junk crowding his thoughts—or his scene.

Zinsser goes on, "The secret of good writing is to strip every paragraph to its cleanest components." That same secret applies to photography. Every photographer worth his zoom lens whittles to the bone and those who don't will pay the price—flabby photographs.

In short, say one thing at a time, and say it clearly. Pare away the excess. Junk the clutter. Strip the fat. Clutter dilutes, confuses, and muddles. Get rid of it.

How do you get rid of clutter? Change viewpoint, moving in closer or higher or to the side. Change lenses, using a telephoto to narrow the view. Move the subject, shifting it to a location free of distractions. If nothing works, abandon the subject and find a new one.

Shown on the next page are several ways of isolating a subject.

One of the delights of children is that they squirm and tease and can't hold still—yet adults often suppress the spontaneity of children when photographing them. Relax, when things don't go as you want, photograph them as they are.

Dan Curtis

1. *Simple surroundings.* If the surroundings are simple, then only the subject will attract attention. Look for a plain foreground, or exclude the foreground and find a plain background. Exclude unnecessary objects.

2. *Full frame.* By filling the frame with the subject, you make it the only thing to view. You can fill the frame by moving in close or by using a telephoto lens.

3. *Selective focus.* When you can't exclude the surroundings, you can use selective focus to render them out of focus and only the subject in focus. Selective focus is most easily achieved by using a telephoto lens at a large aperture like f/3.5. You should also use it at close to medium focusing distances. Check in your viewfinder to see how blurry extraneous objects look.

4. *Tonal contrast.* When the subject is brightly lit against a dark background or silhouetted against a light background, it stands out. If tonal contrast doesn't exist naturally, sometimes you can create it by using your flash to brighten up the subject and separate it from the background.

5. *Color contrast.* When the subject is differently colored from its surroundings, it becomes more noticeable. Color contrast usually works best when the contrast is between bright and muted colors and not simply between bright contrasting colors which compete for attention.

COMPOSITION

Composition has been around as long as art, and probably longer, beginning when some prehistoric person grunted, "Don't you like it better over here?" and dragged the mammoth skin across the cave.

The question posed by our mammoth-skin decorator wasn't really a question but an opinion. That's all composition is, an opinion, an opinion of how a given scene looks best.

Edward Weston's opinion was that "composition is the strongest way of seeing." Weston undoubtedly knew there are as many ways of composing as there are subjects, as there are photographers seeing the subject. The best composition is the one that works.

Many books try to formulate the "strongest way of seeing," and many photographers rigidly adhere to those formulations. The books prescribe the rule of thirds, and photographers, thinking they've read gospel, plot an imaginary grid onto the scene seeking to place subjects at the thirds. The books talk about finding a center of interest, and the photographers find that center of interest and following the books again, keep that center of interest away from the center.

By all means read about and study composition, and become familiar with creating balance and imbalance, a sense of proportion, and how they can alter the mood of a given composition. But don't string rules on a key chain with the thought you can ap-

proach any subject and open the door to perfect composition with a rule.

Instead think first of your subject and your intentions. Then think of lines, shapes, colors, rhythms and meanings, and sift through the possible compositions to find the one that feels right.

Like a worn shoe, composition should almost be unnoticeable. The best composition is the one that's most appealing, and what is most appealing often depends on the subject and circumstances.

Jack Ward/The Image Bank

To go with the flow of the hills running downward, the photographer placed the tree at the left where the hills bottom out.

To the photographer, the three white subjects in the scene below begged for triangular arrangement. The photographer yielded by moving the dog so it was centered beneath the windows.

Camera, lenses, film

Since you use a camera, a lens, and film to photograph, you need to understand how they see differently from you and how those differences affect your photographs. Here are some of the ways in which they see differently: the camera indiscriminately includes everything within its view; it sees the world inside a rectangle; it sees a slice of time carved by the shutter; it sees varying perspectives according to viewpoint.

W. H. M. J. Vander Horst

DETAIL

The first way your camera sees differently is that it doesn't really see at all. Not a glimmer, not a jot, not one iota. Seeing means sensation, which is absent in the camera; it means a living being simmering with conscious and subconscious wants that direct the eye to reconnoiter the way to the rest room or to find the chocolate ice cream in the freezer.

Like a rock on the beach, the camera gets splashed by every image coming its way. It can't select. That's your job. So when you find something to photograph, you must shift from your selective viewing to the camera's nonselective viewing. You must look into the viewfinder and see everything there to see because if you don't, the camera will. It will include lawn chairs, tricycles, and all the clutter you overlooked.

The camera's amazing ability to capture detail isn't always a liability. Often it's an asset. Copious detail, bountiful detail, armfuls of detail that the eye on its own could never hold is one of the camera's fortes.

Keep your eye out for those scenes and subjects bulging with congruent detail, for detail that amazes and amuses. When you find it, use a fine-grained film like KODACHROME 25 or KODACOLOR VR 100 and a small f-stop to hold that detail.

Above, unlike human vision which tends to concentrate on things of interest, camera and film see everything within the field of the lens. Until you also learn to see everything within the field of view and exclude the extraneous, you will get much more detail than you want.

Right, just as the eye tends to skim over unwanted detail so does it tend to skim over desirable detail—except in a photograph. When you find a scene rich with details, such as these dried flowers you can best hold those details by using an extremely fine-grained film like KODACHROME 64 or KODACOLOR VR 100 Film.

THE FRAME

If you were to hold your eye perfectly steady, an unnatural state, you would find the human eye has a frame—a roughly elliptical border defined by the bony orbits around the eye. But since your eye normally flicks about a scene, it is in effect unbounded.

But a photograph has boundaries, and in forming a frame those boundaries do things you should consider. They exclude and include things. They orient things top and bottom, left and right. They make shapes with the images. They enlarge space or shrink it.

Photography writers have made it a practice to include instructions with the frame. They tell you about balancing the image within the frame, about orienting the frame vertically or horizontally to accommodate vertical or horizontal subjects, about leveling the frame, about not squeezing subjects into corners. This is traditional advice. Traditionally it is followed. Usually it works.

But don't let tradition inhibit you from manipulating the frame to see the effects of different variations. Angle subjects from the corners or sides. Tilt the frame. Squeeze a face into the corner and see if it seems scrunched. Is the effect appropriate to the subject? Used badly, unusual framing may seem affected, but bad is one of the steps on the way to good, so welcome it and be on your way.

It is the nature of picture borders to include and exclude. But in this picture they do it dramatically. Such a close cropping of this woman's face violates normal human personal space and would seem painfully intimate were not the eyes excluded.

Mark Cohen

Alone and sitting on the end of the bench, this person seems isolated. The photographer heightened the isolation by placing the person at the edge of the frame. Our line of vision is down the middle of the picture, and the bench sitter is almost ignored.

This motorboat was panned at twilight using a shutter speed of 1 second.

Motion exists all about us and is often best translated by a slow shutter speed that blurs the motion. How much blur occurs depends upon subject speed and shutter speed. Here a shutter speed of 1/8 second was used.

SHUTTER AND MOTION

The shutter enables the camera to capture motion in ways unseen by the eye. The closest thing a person has to a shutter, and it's not very close, is an eyelid whose blink is solely for window washing. A shutter, depending on its speed, can stop motion, let it collect as a blur, or not even let it register. On the other hand, the eye can do little more than note the existence of a moving subject and track it. It is unable to net individual moments from the flux or to freeze the blur in one image as does the camera.

Since the photographer can't scrutinize a moving subject and since reflexes may dally, the more pictures you take, the more likely you'll get a good image. Like chasing a butterfly with your bare hands, it takes a lot of tries to make a catch. Even in something as unmoving as portrait photography where only expressions shift, photographers often expose an entire roll to get one picture with the right expression.

Sharpness results from a shutter speed fast enough to freeze motion. Blur results from a shutter speed too slow to freeze motion. Blur, the obvious representative of motion, smears nose and eyes, dissolves legs, sprouts extra heads—effects that happen only on film.

Sharpness reveals shapes, forms, and details, and indicates motion only if the subject shows a posture uncommon to the resting position. In other words, shown sharp, something inflexible like a race car will be perceived as moving only if it's somersaulting through the air. Something flexible like a person gesturing can be perceived as moving because the gesture does not belong to a person at rest.

Blur has many spinoffs. You can hold the camera steady and let the subject smear across the film. You can move the camera to blur an un-

83

Luis A. Hueso

A slight amount of blur in the dashing girls gives a sense of urgency to their movements.

*Action stopped, **below,** is recognizable as action only if the subjects are caught in poses distinctly different from their appearances at rest.*

moving subject. You can pan the camera with a moving subject to keep the subject fairly sharp and blur the background. For panning, the camera is normally moved smoothly and straight, but interesting results occur if it is jerked or panned as if it were a roller coaster, or if a very slow shutter speed (1/4 second or slower) is used.

Most of us relegate motion photography to big things meant to move quickly—things like cars, motorcycles, and joggers. Everyday motion we overlook. Have you ever photographed a door swinging shut, a child sliding out of bed, daffodils dancing in the wind? If not, begin now. Explore everyday motion. Mouths open, curtains flutter, brooms sweep, feet fidget, faucets flow. Make a list of the possibilities. Use a tripod and a slow shutter speed like 1/4 second to blur any motion.

Harry McDonald, Sr.

84

Glenn Morgan

Instead of waiting for the sunbather to pose prettily for the camera, the photographer caught her tangled in her sundress. The white sundress plays nicely against the clouds as does the rectangle of the blanket against the rectangle of the beach, against the rectangle of the water.

WHEN TO PRESS THE SHUTTER

When to press the shutter—a simple contraction of the index finger whose timing means little to still lifes but much to objects in motion. Before pressing the shutter, photographers have traditionally waited. For what? For the scene in flux to arrive at an ideal moment, a moment when subjects are balanced and arranged in a compositionally pleasing manner, for the pedestrian to emerge from behind the telephone pole and the motorcyclist to fully enter the frame. Then they pressed the shutter.

But such pictures are not so much pictures of flux as they are pictures of composition. Was it not composition that determined when the picture was taken? Pleasing to view, compositional pictures of flux present a conventional although somewhat distorted view of reality. If you were to randomly freeze the flux of a scene, you'd not find an idealistic composition but an awkward posturing of people caught rising from park benches, faces buried in handkerchiefs, and cars bisected by the frame's borders. It would be like arriving unannounced at a friend's house where instead of the usual spic-and-span housekeeping, you see shoes and newspapers strewn across the floor and dirty dishes on the table.

Showing the awkwardness of flux is showing a view seldom photographed. Of course, once it becomes commonplace it loses its power of surprise. Ironically, capturing the reality of flux isn't done simply by randomly snapping the shutter but by carefully waiting until subjects reach that "ideal" awkwardness. Even the so-called realistic view requires a carefully timed shot that simulates what the photographer believes to represent flux.

LENSES

There are a lot of lenses. But none is more popular than the four-element, 17 mm lens with automatic focus and automatic diaphragm ranging from f/3 to f/12, with a vertical viewing angle of 140° and a horizontal angle of 180°, and with a built-in lens shade and internal color correction. Like it? You have one, two actually—your eyes.

But if your eyes should roll down the conveyor to the quality control inspector of a lens manufacturer, they'd get tossed into the reject pile. They just aren't up to snuff. Compared to modern lenses designed by computers and made with rare earth elements, your eyes are cracked marbles that can't roll straight let alone see straight. Too short, too long, too warped, they work nonetheless. You have lived with them, defects and all, and they have made the world familiar in their way.

Their way. Your impressions of the world depend in part on the images formed by your eyes as lenses. Other lenses form different images, thus show the world in other ways. Given sharpness and speed, the ways of lenses important to photography are focal length, focus, and depth of field.

The most common and most important use of lenses is simply to fit the image you want onto the film: a wide-angle lens to include all of the ocean liner QE II, a telephoto lens to magnify a distant windsurfer.

But lenses can also alter the appearance of a scene. For practical purposes, lenses of different focal lengths can often change apparent perspective. (Technically, only shooting distance changes the perspective.) Perspective is the way three-dimensional space is rendered on two-dimensional paper. A lens can appear to magnify, stretch, or shrink space.

First, you must train yourself to become aware of how focal length in conjunction with subject distance can alter perspective. Then you must train yourself to recognize when you want to alter perspective.

Of the three categories of lenses, wide-angle, normal, and telephoto, normal lenses (40-60 mm for 35 mm cameras) yield a perspective similar to that given by the eye. That's why they're called normal lenses.

M. J. Guariglia

24 mm lens

50 mm lens

200 mm lens

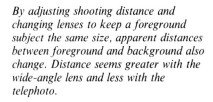

By adjusting shooting distance and changing lenses to keep a foreground subject the same size, apparent distances between foreground and background also change. Distance seems greater with the wide-angle lens and less with the telephoto.

Different lenses let you vary the way you see things. Some let you see closer, some further. But more important than a lens' optical idiosyncrasy, such as wide-angle distortion which often appears gimmicky, is that a lens enables you to obtain and frame the image you want.

By using a wide-angle lens and including a fence running from foreground to background, the photographer was able to stress the distance.

WIDE-ANGLE LENSES

With wide-angle lenses you can increase the sense of space and distances between things when photographing nearby subjects. The shorter the focal length, the greater the exaggeration of space. To alter apparent perspective noticeably, include close subjects as well as medium or distant subjects.

Close subjects appear fairly normal or slightly large in size, while farther subjects are much smaller. The size differentiation between near and far things causes the space exaggeration.

Although you can use wide-angle lenses to make portrait caricatures or to elongate skyscrapers, such special effects are obvious whereas the subtler effects of expanded space can appear normal, yet create a strong feeling of depth in a picture. By careful selection and juxtaposition of near and far subjects, you can shift the emphasis from distance to size. For instance, you can turn a foreground dandelion into a sequoia towering over a background person (see page 55). Emphasizing unusual size relationships generally requires a 28 mm or shorter focal length lens and a small aperture like f/16 to give sufficient depth of field.

Although the steeples are nearly half a mile from the skyscraper behind them, the photographer was able to make them appear stacked upon one another by using a 300 mm telephoto lens.

TELEPHOTO LENSES

Unlike wide-angle lenses, telephoto lenses compress apparent distances between things. The longer the focal length, the greater the compression. The effect becomes especially noticeable with lenses longer than 200 mm. The apparent compression results from the narrow field of view.

To shorten distances between things noticeably, you need to work with subjects at medium-far to far distances. Making things appear closer together may at first seem to have little value, but with a little thought you can imagine situations where a more crowded feeling would be appropri-ate. Photographed through a normal lens, strollers on Fifth Avenue may appear to be having a mid-afternoon walk. But when photographed through a 500 mm lens you are thrust into a crowd ready to trample stragglers. The number of people doesn't change, the 500 mm lens just seems to bunch them together. Jamming things together can drastically alter mood.

More subtly, lessening distances between things tightens the relationship between them. The closer they are, the more apparent it is they are together, even if they aren't. To maintain this togetherness, the principal subjects would have to be rendered sharp. That can be a problem with telephoto lenses. A small f-stop like f/16 is required.

Small f-stops often mean slow shutter speeds. With telephoto lenses, slow shutter speeds can lead to blur. To avoid blur, use a tripod or a fast film. KODACOLOR VR 200 Film, ISO 200, and KODACOLOR VR 400 Film, ISO 400, work well with telephoto lenses. Both have extremely fine grain. Both are fast enough to give high shutter speeds under a variety of lighting conditions.

André Martin

Left, André Martin is well known for his romantic interpretations. As in this picture, he often uses long telephoto lenses at large apertures to produce a small area of sharpness—otherwise known as selective focus. Here a 300 mm lens was set at f/4.5.

Lower left, seeing one sharp image from foreground to background is beyond the limits of the human eye. But a lens used at a small aperture like f/22 can make an image sharp from foreground to background.

DEPTH OF FIELD

Many pictures are made with an intermediate f-stop like f/8 that gives a gradation from sharpness to unsharpness. With an f-stop at either extreme, however, that gradation is typically absent and its absence becomes noticeable.

The largest f-stop (often f/1.8) gives the shallowest depth of field. The smallest f-stop (often f/16) gives the greatest depth of field.

Large f-stops can be used to achieve selective focus so only the subject appears sharp. Foreground and background blur. Selective focus is further aided by using a telephoto lens and focusing on a near subject.

Great depth of field making both foreground and background sharp is achieved using a wide-angle or normal lens at a small f-stop. Use the depth-of-field scale or previewer to gauge the depth of field for a given aperture. Sharpness in both foreground and background can be achieved only photographically.

*The camera's viewing image, **top,** is provided by the lens' largest aperture (typically f/1.8) whereas the picture image, **above,** is provided by whatever aperture you select. What appeared unsharp and subdued in the viewfinder may be sharp and distracting in the picture even if you use an aperture only two or three stops smaller than the largest aperture. This is most evident when photographing things closer than 10 ft (3m) or using a telephoto lens.*

FILM

Film reacts to light. How it reacts to light affects the appearance of a photograph. The most basic reaction of films is that some films produce color photographs and others produce black-and-white photographs.

Since it does not show color, black-and-white film steps away from reality. Color is everywhere—your shoes, your car, your rug. It's impossible to overlook. So why do black-and-white photographers overlook color? Because it is everywhere and impossible not to overlook. And often, color is simply unattractive, ruining an otherwise good picture. Moreover, black-and-white photographers find color overbearing, a distraction, a tease from what is really important. To them what is important is tone, form,

shape, texture, meaning, and by deleting color, they can concentrate on those elements. Plus, some photographers simply like the look of black-and-white better than color.

Color photographers like color. They like it because it is colorful and appealing. They like it because color photographs are more representative of reality. Humans see color; therefore, they reason, photographs should show color. Color photographers also often find bright colors distracting but they work to subordinate color to their intent.

Neither color nor black-and-white film responds to light exactly as does the eye. Different color films, especially slide films, reproduce colors slightly differently. Some films give warmer colors, some give cooler col-

You may find it useful to switch to black-and-white film when form, texture, composition, lighting and the many other elements in a scene are strong but color is not. KODAK Technical Pan Film was used here because of its extremely fine grain.

ors. Warmer color-balanced films are often chosen to photograph people. Cooler color-balanced films may be used for flowers or landscapes.

You don't normally think of black-and-white films responding to color, but they do. They show colors in tones. Since you can't see in black and white, seeing colors as tones becomes a matter of experience and study. To prevent tones from blending, filters are used. In the photograph, a filter generally lightens tones from colors similar to those of the filter and darkens tones from other colors.

Black-and-white film is more sensitive to blue light and ultraviolet radiation than the eye. Since the sky is the most obvious source of blue light and ultraviolet radiation, it appears too light if not filtered. By using a No. 8 yellow filter, the sky appears normal. No. 15 deep yellow, No. 21 orange, and No. 25 red filters considerably darken the sky by blocking blue light and ultraviolet radiation. For more on filtering black-and-white films, see *Using Filters*, KW-13, or *Advanced B/W Photography*, KW-19.

Another characteristic of film is graininess, the sand-like appearance

Of course, only color film can give color pictures. So when the colors in a scene are important to you, use color film.

of film apparent at great enlargements. Graininess typically increases with film speed. A slow-speed film like KODACHROME 25, ISO 25, has much finer grain than a very high-speed film like KODACOLOR VR 1000, ISO 1000. Even with very high-speed films, grain often does not become apparent until big enlargements are made.

If you want to step away from reality by adding graininess, you can use a high-speed film and greatly enlarge it. Graininess can add a romantic, dreamy effect to photographs. Or, depending on subject matter, it can reinforce a breaking-up of reality.

To best achieve grainy effects, use a

fast film. Graininess can be further stressed by push-processing film and greatly enlarging the image. For black-and-white photographs, KODAK Recording Film 2475 is a good choice. It has a coarse grain that can be accented by pushing the film up to ISO 3200. For color photographs you could greatly enlarge KODACOLOR VR 1000 Film (it can't be push processed) but might get better results using a high-speed EKTACHROME Film. EKTACHROME Films can be push processed.

The pictures on page 93 were shot on EKTACHROME 400 Film, ISO 400, rated at ISO 1600 and push-processed 2 stops. If you can't find a photofin-

isher who pushes EKTACHROME 400 Film 2 stops, you can do it yourself using a KODAK HOBBY-PAC Color Slide Kit. Or you could rate it at ISO 800 and push it 1 stop by asking your dealer for Kodak processing and a KODAK Special Processing Envelope, ESP-1.

Another alternative is to use KODAK EKTACHROME P800/1600 Professional Film. It can be rated at ISO 800 or ISO 1600 and gives better colors and shadow densities than pushed EKTACHROME 400 Film. Tell your photofinisher what film speed you used and ask for the appropriate KODAK Special Processing Envelope.

Often considered a drawback, film grain can also be used advantageously to reinforce a mood. At right, it conveys the delicacy of this high-key scene and below it strengthens the sense of Saturday morning mayhem. Both shots, enlarged 6x, were made by rating KODAK EKTACHROME 400 Film at ISO 1600 and having it push-processed two stops during development. Similar but less grainy results could be obtained by rating EKTACHROME 400 Film at ISO 800 and asking your photodealer to process it using a Kodak Special Processing Envelope, ESP-1, or by greatly enlarging a negative from KODACOLOR VR 1000 Film.

2. The cornea, a curved transparent window at the front of the eye, strongly bends light. Behind the cornea, the lens changes its curvature to focus images of subjects at different distances. The iris, the colored part of the eye, functions like an aperture diaphragm, narrowing in bright light and widening in dim light. The pupil is the aperture through which light enters the eye. The eye does not see. It only forms images of light on the retina. The retina electrically codes those images and transmits them to the brain.

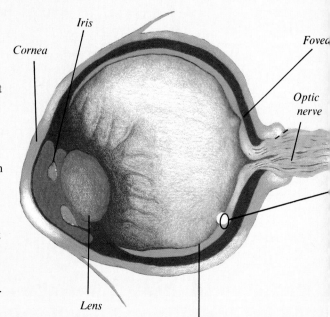

Iris
Cornea
Fovea
Optic nerve
Lens
Retina

1. Vision begins with light entering the eye.

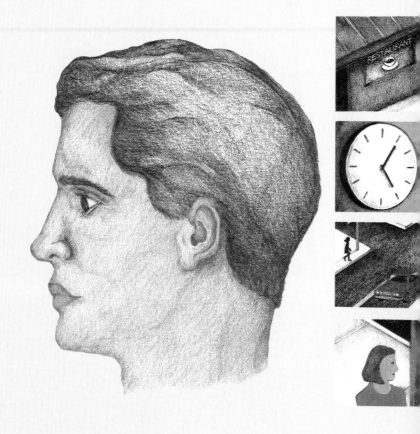

Retina

Nerve cell

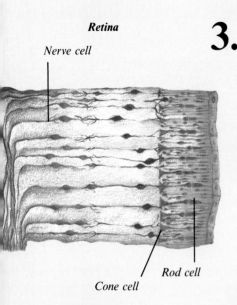

Cone cell

Rod cell

3. The retina, lining the inside of the eyeball, senses incoming light. As an outgrowth of the brain, the retina makes the eye the only sense organ that is part of the brain. The retina has two types of light-sensitive cells: rod cells and cone cells. Rod cells function mainly in dim light and give black-and-white vision. Cone cells function in bright light and give color vision.

Before light reaches the retina, it passes through blood vessels and nerve cells that filter out 90 percent of the entering light. The area of sharpest vision in the retina is the fovea. It contains 35,000 cone cells and no rod cells. Nerve cells and blood vessels skirt around the fovea to give free entry of light. The fovea is only 1/50 inch in diameter. Within the fovea, each cone cell connects to a single bipolar nerve cell to give high resolution. Outside the fovea, each bipolar nerve cell connects to several cone cells, giving lower resolution.

The image formed on the retina is small, upside down, and moves with each flick of the eye or nod of the head.

4.

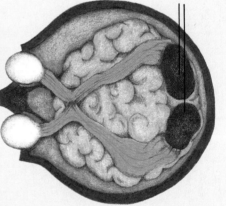

Visual cortex

Although seeing occurs within the brain, seeing is not a direct representation of the retinal image. Before reaching the brain, electrical signals have been edited and interpreted by nerve cells and relay centers. The signals reaching the brain are handed out to different areas of the visual cortex. The arrangement of the visual cortex may represent a spatial relation to the retina. Specific cells and sometimes specific columns of cells respond to certain colors, contours, line orientations, and movement. Other cells react more generally--any line and a variety of colors may cause them to respond. From these data, the brain builds a model of reality. We see.

5. What we see and how we see is not strictly a matter of physiological responses. Some visual nerve cells may have memory that responds to certain lines and shapes previously seen (recognition). Other responses are determined by past experiences (knowledge) of sizes, shapes, and distances. And the very things we see depend in large part on our emotions. The hungry person sees the sign for a restaurant. The person late for an appointment sees a clock. The tired person may not actually see, but only maneuver through sidewalk and street traffic. And almost always, the brain does not respond to every part of the image formed on the retina but selects the one or two important to it at the moment. To attend to all the images striking the retina would be exhausting.

Recommended reading

The Art of Photography, Editors of TIME-LIFE Books, TIME-LIFE Books, Alexandria, Virginia. 1971.

Eye and Brain, R. L. Gregory, McGraw-Hill Book Company, New York, New York. 1977.

Eye, Film, and Camera in Color Photography, Ralph M. Evans, John Wiley & Sons, Inc., New York, New York. 1959.

Looking at Photographs, John Szarkowski, Museum of Modern Art, New York, New York. 1973.

More Joy of Photography, Editors of Eastman Kodak Company, Addison-Wesley Publishing Company, Reading, Massachusetts. 1981.

Photographic Lighting: Learning to See, Ralph Hattersley, Prentice Hall, Inc., Englewood Cliffs, New Jersey. 1979

Photographic Seeing, Andreas Feininger, Prentice-Hall, Englewood Cliffs, New Jersey. 1973.

Photography and the Art of Seeing, Freeman Patterson, Van Nos Reinhold Ltd., Toronto, Ontario. 1979.

Technique of Photographic Lighting, Norm Kerr, Amphoto Books, Garden City, New York. 1979.

Visual Concepts for Photographers, L. Stroebel et al, Focal Press, Inc., New York, New York. 1980.

Index